To Steve

Alone with God

100 Visits with the Father

Alex Zanazanian   8/8/22

The Lord continue
To Bless You in
every area of Your
Life

Alex Zanaz
Ps 139:14-17

Printed in the United States of America

First Printing, 2017

ISBN 13: 978-1979245845
ISBN-10: 1979245843

Acknowledgments

I would like to thank anyone who in any way influenced my life and the path that I have followed. Pastor Ken Stutts on the move into Florida; my pastor, Bishop Mark Chironna; Gregory Griffith, who produced a You Tube video on my life and consistently asked, "How is the book coming?"

Many others touched my life: Joy Mauger, Jennifer Casebier, Susan Singer, Sandra Martin, Pastor Charles Cooker, Pastor Tommy Zukoski, Candice Beland Donna Scuderi, Pastors Brad and Alice Gillman, and last but not least, my daughter, Deborah Hilewick. Each in their own way encouraged me to continue to journal and let the world in on it. I am greatly indebted to God and to them. Thank you.

ALONE WITH GOD

Endorsements

From the beginning, it was about relationship with God. Relationship only develops through relating to each other! I have had the privilege of knowing Alex for many years now. At times, I have also 'listened' alongside him as he was in dialogue with the Lord.   Always in agreement with the Scriptures and the witness of the Holy Spirit, I have been richly blessed by what the Lord has shared with him during those times. Though the conversations are deeply personal between Alex and Abba Father, I know you will also be encouraged and edified as you read this book. May it ultimately inspire you to 'listen' to the Father's voice and draw you into that deeper place of relationship as well!

Sandy Martin
King's Way Ministries, Director
The Church at King's Way, Pastor

From the 1st day Alex let me read and listen to him read these love letters to and from God I was truly amazed. These letters are truly uplifting, inspirational and they physically move in the Holy Spirit. As I kept reading the pages just turned with ease, and kept me intoxicated with our Father and how much He LOVES us. This is without a doubt one of God's masterpieces destined for a brand-new type of daily devotional.

Way to go Alex, proud of you and His work He has given you!!!

Michael Gahan,
Missionary for God in the Philippines making a global impact.

Alex Zanazanian invites you on an intimate journey into the Throne Room of God where hearts are exposed to His presence and sweet communion takes place with the Father. Alex chronicles conversations he has with God and God's responses back to him. Each devotional reflects God's love for His people and His desire for a very personal relationship. You will find the writings profound, deep and thought provoking. Yet, at the same time the reader feels the comfort and joy found in the presence of a loving Heavenly Father.
**In His service and co-laboring to build His Kingdom,
Pastor Beverly Lorenz**

I will always cherish the many mornings where I would have the opportunity to hear the intimate words between God and His loyal son Alex over coffee. Although these moments were shared between God and Alex, I always felt as though God was speaking straight to me as Alex would share his journal writings with me. What a blessing it is that Alex's visits with God can now be shared with so many more. May the words on these pages touch the hearts of all who read and draw each and every person closer to Christ. If anyone wonders what God's love looks like, keep reading and you will surely see. Thank you Alex for being His vessel and sharing His love and messages with us.
Candice Beland

Foreword

I met Alex for the first time in 2009. Our paths would cross from time to time, but never to the magnitude they would in 2013. When Alex's wife Nancy went home to be with the Lord, I saw some things that Alex was carrying that I just knew I wanted. I reached out to him and we planned to meet for lunch. Little did I know that this 4-hour lunch would change my life. I felt like Mitch Albom in the book, "Tuesday's with Morrie. "

Alex was opening my eyes up to a whole new world that could only be understood by someone who had enjoyed the Journey the way Alex had. As we spent more time together over the past 4 years, our lives would both be strengthened and changed by this relationship God had ordained. I am Honored and Blessed to have Alex in my life.

These letters to God are the equivalent of being in Alex's prayer chamber with him. If you ever wondered how to have a relationship with God, Alex will teach you in this book. Alex understands how valuable relationships are, and he shows us that the most important relationship is with God. Alex has tapped into The Source, and the best thing we can do is to follow his lead.

You will be encouraged and strengthened by reading this book. This book will help take you to unfamiliar places in your walk with Jesus. This book will stretch you and challenge you daily. Alone with God is a masterpiece. I recommend you buy multiple copies and give it to everyone you know.

Pastor Brad Gillman
Hearts of Fire Ministries

CONTENTS

Introduction

The following pages are reflections of my visits with my heavenly Father. Always, our time together is deeply personal, because He is a Person, divine and relational.

One hundred visits are divided into seven sections. In the first section, the worshiper thanks and praises God. In keeping with the mandate to "enter His gates with thanksgiving and His courts with praise" (Ps. 100:4 NASB), readers can begin their devotions with a page from this section. In the remaining sections, the Father speaks as only He can, to enlighten, encourage, and empower His child. In all cases, Scripture references and closing questions are also included, to encourage personal reflection and deeper intimacy with God.

The conversations contained in these pages will resonate with committed Christ followers and invite the uninitiated into relationship with God, through the saving work of His Son, Jesus Christ. The following prayer is offered for those who desire to take a step toward the Savior:

> *Dear Father in heaven, please reveal Yourself to me in the coming pages. Lead me into Your truth and into an abiding relationship with You, through Your Son, and by Your Holy Spirit. Amen.*

May this book strengthen and comfort you as the goodness of the Creator is revealed.

Alex Zanazanian

ରଡ ରଡ ରଡ

Giving Thanks and Praise

God is our tender, loving, able, affirming, trustworthy, truthful, forgiving, compassionate, caring, providing, healing, listening, answering, and everlasting Father. Always present, now and forever, He brings nothing but good all the days of our lives. Through every mountaintop and valley experience, He guides us onward and proves Himself faithful.

Our Father is worthy of our praise and worship! Continually, He seeks to reconcile us to Himself, even when we stray from Him. When we follow Him, we see His power and might fulfilling His plans for us, more and more. He offers us His listening ear and promises to grant the desires of our hearts. Never does He fail His own!

He is our God, our glorious and wondrous Lord. In His magnificent presence, we are awestruck. May He be blessed as we thank and praise Him throughout this section, for He is worthy!

1 John 4:8, Eph. 4:32, Ps. 103:8, 2 Cor. 5:18–19

ରଡ ରଡ ରଡ

ဢ   ဢ   ဢ

Father's Heart

Lord, thank You for rescuing me from the kingdom of darkness and adopting me into Your family. You are my faithful Abba Father and I am Your child, redeemed with Your love, once and forever. My never-failing Father, You promised never to leave me. Your promise is trustworthy! Therefore, I bless You with the thanksgiving and praise only You are worthy to receive. Thank You, dear Father! Praise You, my Lord, for receiving me with open arms and welcoming me into Your house and heart. Thank You for Your extreme, undying faithfulness and for Your mercies that are new every morning. Thank You for undergirding me, lifting me up, and giving me peace, tranquility, and strength. Thank You that, whatever the situation, You choose to see me through Your eyes of love. Thank You, Father, for making Your presence tangible in Your faithfulness. Thank You, my King. Thank You!

Col. 1:13, Rom. 8:15, Heb. 13:5, 2 Cor. 1:20, Lam. 3:22–23

Which aspects of the Father's heart touch your own heart most powerfully today?

4

౭ఎ ౭ఎ ౭ఎ

Heart of Thanksgiving

Father, I am moved by the gratitude of those who see Your goodness in the land of the living, even when they are suffering. From the bottom of my heart, I thank You for the freedom and sustenance You provide. I can worship You amid hardship because You endue me with faith, hope, and victory, in spite of ordeals. The more I thank You, the more joy, happiness, and fulfillment I experience. Thank You, Father, for everything You are and all You do! Like those who have gone before me, I choose to be thankful in every circumstance. As I offer the thanks and praise You deserve, You reveal even more of Your love for me. Thank You for rejoicing my heart with gladness and peace! I will continue to bless You at all times. Thank You, Father, for providing all things that pertain to life and godliness. Thank You, Lord. I will thank You and thank You, always!

Ps. 27:13, Hab. 3:17–18, 1 Thess. 5:16–18,
Ps. 95:2, 107:22, 2 Pet. 1:3

Is yours an attitude of gratitude? How do you express your gratitude to God?

ဆ   ဆ   ဆ

Thank You for the Cross

Heavenly Father, thank You for loving us so much that You gave Your Son to save us! Thank You for the resurrection power that raised Him from the dead and left the tomb empty! How grateful I am that He overcame hell and death forever. I am soberly aware and deeply humbled that the living Christ, who is now seated at Your right hand, is the ultimate example of overcoming every obstacle and arising victorious! Because He was obedient, I can be obedient, however difficult or distressing my situation might be. Jesus' perfect obedience pleased You and freed me to do the same. Because He laid down His life, I was brought, by the power of the Holy Spirit, into the sweetness of relationship that You and He share! Thank You for this amazing and matchless gift! How it fills my heart with Your glory and satisfies me in Your presence! It is beyond the capacity of my human understanding.

John 3:16, Matt. 17:22-23, Rev. 1:18, Col. 3:1,
John 17:21, 1 Cor. 2:9

Have you accepted the work of the cross as a sacrifice made on your behalf?

6

ಲ ಲ ಲ

Gracious God

God, You are truly awesome and beyond comprehension, yet You reveal Yourself as the personal God who discloses His heart and discerns my every thought. You bring forth the sweet fruit of righteousness that satisfies and makes me content. Thank You, my gracious heavenly Father! Thank You for drawing me close and securing me in Your embrace. Thank You, Abba Father, for affirming me with words of love, joy, and peace. Even in uncertain times, You assure me that You are here with me. Blessed are You, and so deserving of my trust! Reveal Yourself more and more so that I may know Your full glory and splendor. My God, I adore and worship You. I bow down before You in praise, honor, and glory, magnifying Your mighty name. You are Christ Jesus, the King of kings and Lord of lords, the first and the last, my Lord and my Master. I thank You!

Rom. 11:33, 1 Cor. 2:10, 1 Sam. 16:7, Heb. 4:12,
Ps. 36:5, Exod. 33:18

How has God been gracious to you? Which signs of His goodness might you be overlooking?

ഗ ഗ ഗ

Dear Abba

Father, I am so aware of Your steady, watchful eye. Thank You for being the everlasting God who neither slumbers nor sleeps, my Abba Father who cares for me so tenderly. I give thanks for Your heart of love and forgiveness. Though You are true, just, and holy, You have compassion for my frailties. I am ever on Your mind and in Your heart. Perhaps Your greatest desire is for me to know the details of Your perfect Fatherhood. May my eyes be open, Lord, and if they are not, search my heart! See if there is any wicked way in me and I will gladly confess it so You can heal my soul. Thank You, Father, for restoring me so we can celebrate our life together. You alone are worthy. You alone deserve all the glory. You alone are God and Creator, victorious in all things. You are my God and I am Your child, now and forever. Thank You, Father, for Your precious love!

Gen. 21:33, Ps. 121:4, Gal. 4:6, Heb. 4:15,
Ps. 139:23–24, Rev. 4:11

What astounds you most about the Father's care of you?

ဢ   ဢ   ဢ

My Restorer

Father, thank You for restoring the lost years of my life and the opportunities I missed in past seasons. Because of the finished work of the cross, I can recover the promises and blessings that slipped away from me. You have given me the power to pursue, overtake, and recover my goods from my enemies. In Jesus' name and because of Your goodness, I cancel every curse and demonic assignment that was set against me and what You have promised me. Thank You for giving me the power of a new beginning. Thank You for making my life a miracle. Thank You for being glorified in every area of my life. Thank You for divine solutions to every challenge I face. Thank You for causing my enemies to flee from me in seven directions. Thank You for a sevenfold restoration and recovery in every area of my life. Thank You, Father, Son, and Holy Spirit for receiving my praise and answering my prayer!

1 Sam. 30:8, Isa. 54:17, James 1:5, Deut. 28:7, Prov. 6:31

What kind of restoration do you need? Will you ask Your Father for it?

❧ ❧ ❧

Majestic and Knowable God

Awesome God, You are mighty in power! You reign supreme as the sovereign God who is above all others. You are the majestic God of eternity past, future, and forever. Your kingdom will never end. By the words of Your mouth—"Let it be!"—You brought the universe into existence and said it was good. Thank You for creating it and us with Your unlimited imagination and unending creativity. There is no one like You. You are holy and perfect in every way. You are merciful, loving, kind, gracious, compassionate, and faithful. Yes! You are all of this and more. I cannot comprehend the vastness of You. There is so much mystery and yet You are *my Father* who allows Himself to be known. Thank You for inviting me to search Your heart. Thank You for the true and beautiful relationship we share. You are my best friend, my forever partner. For all of this, I thank and praise You!

1 Tim. 1:17, Luke 1:33, Gen. 1:3-26,
John 17:3, Jer. 29:12-13

How is God inviting you to know Him more?

ॐ   ॐ   ॐ

So, So Good!

Lord, You are *so* good that I cannot fathom the breadth of Your goodness. You are faithful and trustworthy, my never-failing God. Your wisdom and justice are perfect. You are a bulwark in every storm. You are my source, my rock, my foundation. Your arms enfold me, holding me close to Your heart, where I hear Your sweet whisper. When I am troubled, You say, "Don't worry. I am with you." O the calm that comes when Your voice pierces the quietness and makes me freshly aware that You are here! How Your peace settles over me as Your rest floods my being. Thank You for filling my emptiness and making me more pliable each day. Thank You for Your gentleness in conforming me to Your ways. Thank You most of all for sending Your Son, the Word made flesh, to live in me. Thank You, Lord. You are so, so good!

Ps. 23:6, Isa. 25:4, Josh. 1:9, 2 Chron. 20:30, Rom. 8:29

How is God's goodness affecting you right now?

℘   ℘   ℘

The River

Father, thank You for the river of living water that flows from Your heart, saturating my spirit, consciousness, and life. Your life-giving river washes away every blemish and heals the sickness of my soul. It leaves me spotless in Your presence and perfect in Your sight. Thank You! I am desperate for this living water and for Your healing balm that soothes and redeems me! O the glory of Your presence and the freedom You give! Thank You for providing the continuous flow that surges from Your fount! It has been my solace, strength, and peace in every trial through all these years. Your living water is Your gift. It satisfies my thirst and beautifies every step in my journey. Thank You, Lord! Blessed be Your name. Thank You for the river You give so freely to all who will come and drink from it. Thank You, Lord, for it is life to me!

Ps. 46:4, Ps. 105:41, John 7:38, Rev. 22:1

Are you thirsting for the river of living water?

ଋ ଋ ଋ

Your Courage and Humility

My Jesus! What courage You showed at the cross, and what humility! Willing and obedient to perform Your Father's will *to the letter*, You accomplished His eternal purpose and bore the cost of my salvation. This pleased the Father and released the power of redemption throughout Creation. How can I thank You for humbling Yourself and making my redemption possible? Through Your sacrifice, I can live courageously. You have empowered me to submit to You without reservation, to trust You more fully with each passing day. Your courage becomes the strength I need to accomplish whatever You call me to do. Daily, I press on, clutching Your hand and clinging to Your promises. Thank You for the courage to follow You, saying what You tell me to say and going where You tell me to go. My heart and life are in Your hands. Do with them what You will, in Your precious name!

Heb. 12:2, Phil. 2:8, Isa. 1:19, 1 Cor. 1:30, Heb. 10:23

How are Christ's courage and humility seen in your life?

ෆ ෆ ෆ

You Understand Me

Thank You, Lord, for Your work in me. You care for me and my concerns. You *know* me, even to the number of hairs on my head! When You speak to me, You are precise and to the point. Any confusion I experience comes from the uncertainty within *me*. Even after these many years, memories of certain childhood experiences inhibit my ability to trust You fully. Still, Your faithfulness never wavers. Day by day, You reveal how my reasoning quells my faith. You don't berate me for it; You simply speak to me. You know the depths of my inner battles. You help identify my weaknesses. You understand how my reasoning generates anxiety and feeds my fear of the unknown. You know how many times I have fallen into that trap! Yet You never abandon me or condemn me for my foolishness. Ever so gently, You whisper in my heart and remind me that You care. How I thank You!

Luke 12:7, 2 Samuel 22:31, Prov. 3:5, Ps. 139:2, 1 Pet. 5:7

What tormenting thoughts drive your fears today?
Will you lay them at the Father's feet?

ಇ ಇ ಇ

Your Loving-kindness

Thank You, Lord, for the loving-kindness that reaches the depths of my heart and bathes me in Your presence. You are present in the peace and joy You bestow. I breathe of You deeply, satisfying my innermost needs. Thank You for reminding me that You are here and that nothing can separate me from Your love—*nothing*. My past is under the blood of Jesus, and so is my future! Great things are in store; my journey is far from over. Ahead are giants to defeat and increasing light to walk in. You are that light. You lead me beside still waters and cause lush green fields to thrive within me. Because You fill my life, I can testify to Your goodness, *now* in the land of the living! Father, Your loving-kindness is like no other. Thank You! I give You praise and glory now and forevermore.

Ps. 5:7, Heb. 13:5, Rom. 8:38–39, John 8:12,
Ps. 23:2, 27:13

How is God's loving-kindness being demonstrated in your life at this moment?

꙰ ꙰ ꙰

Your Plans for Me

Thank You, Father, for keeping me safe and secure through many trials, and for abiding in me through many seasons. Whether consciously or not, whether I admit it or not, my life has always depended on You, the ultimate source of my well-being. When my heart hardened toward You—when I meandered on strange pathways and clamped my heart shut to Your guidance—You loved me anyway and nudged me toward Your good plan for my life. Through thick and thin, Your love never wavered and Your forgiveness continued to flow! Thank You for giving so graciously to one so undeserving! Thank You for healing and restoring me when my own foolishness invited more suffering. Thank You for drawing me back to Your fold, where every heavenly benefit in Christ Jesus works toward my good and Your purposes. Your plans are *perfect*. Thank You, Father! I praise and adore You, my Master and Lord.

Ps. 27:5, Ps. 16:2, Ps. 56:6, Matt. 18:12, Jer. 29:11, Eph. 1:3

Toward what good plan is the Father nudging you today?

ဢ ဢ ဢ

Thank You for Friends

Lord, You are my all in all, my one and only God who often expresses His love through others. Thank You for the relationships You have granted me. How they enrich my life! Thank You for those You send to encourage me when I'm weary and those who challenge me when I falter in doing or being my best. You have blessed me with family and friends, coworkers and mentors, pastors and other leaders who have loved me, helped me grow, entrusted me with responsibility, and fostered my personal and professional development. I am grateful for their belief in me. They have sown their lives into mine, "polishing" Your image in me and empowering me to walk in Your ways. Help me to remember each and every one of them so that I might pray, "Let Your blessing overtake this amazing and beautiful human being with whom You have graced my life. Amen."

Ps. 16:5, Gen. 2:18, Ps. 68:6, 1 Thess. 5:11,
Prov. 3:12, Eph. 6:18

Consider the people around you and ask the Father to reveal each one's role in your life.

ᏋᏬ   ᏋᏬ   ᏋᏬ

Your Righteousness in Me

Thank You, Father, for imputing Your righteousness to me—a sinner! When I embraced the sacrifice of Your Son and surrendered my life to You, You forgave my sin and empowered me to walk in victory. Always, You have been there, pointing the way and straightening my path. Every day, Your mercy draws me closer. Your forgiveness restores me. Your healing and cleansing power frees me to walk with You. You are a gracious God. Your everlasting love looked beyond my sin and redeemed me. You are my faithful friend and the lover of my soul. Your ways are past finding out, yet You speak to me. As I heed Your voice, You direct my steps. Wonderful heavenly Father, full of grace and truth, You have given me the righteousness I could not earn. Thank You for saving me. Work in me Your plans and purposes. Let Your righteousness in me reveal Your glory in this earth.

Rom. 4:22-24, Prov. 3:6, Ps. 119:156, Rom. 11:33, Ps. 107:2

Are you a disciple of Christ to whom God's righteousness has been imputed? (Please see Preface.)

❧ ❧ ❧

Seeing God as He Is

God is Father, Son, and Holy Spirit. The Father lifts us above the fray and holds us close; the Son died for our sin; the Holy Spirit comes to live inside us. God, our loving Friend, is at the center of all we are and hope to be. He is compassionate, merciful, and forgiving, always encouraging the best in us, and always proving His love to be true and trustworthy, never wavering, always enduring.

We fail Him often, yet He never fails us—never. He forgives us and draws us back to Himself, confirming our place in His heart and proving His desire to receive our love. At times we sense His smile, and know that He is moved by our reverence. When we accept the sacrifice of His dear Son, He promises that nothing will separate us from His love. He is then ours, and we are His, for all eternity. Let Him speak to you in the pages that follow.

Eph. 2:18, John 3:16, Heb. 13:5,
Rom. 8:38-39

❧ ❧ ❧

❧ ❧ ❧

ॐ   ॐ   ॐ

God of All Gods

I am the great *I AM*, both life and breath, the One who indwells you. My creative power formed you and energizes you even now. If You are Mine, that same power dwells *in you*. It is the power of My Spirit flowing, causing you to seek Me and know Me as I really am. Who am I? None other than your Abba Father. Though I transcend logic, You *can* know Me. Truly, I long to reveal Myself to you! So, enter the inner chambers of My heart, where you can experience Me firsthand. Get to know the God of all gods who is preeminent in might and power, who initiates all goodness, and who called all things into being. Come! Feast on My glorious presence. Let it filter in and through you, sustaining and empowering you to call into being things that do not yet exist! Worship, praise, honor, magnify, and exalt My name. Glorify Me by reflecting Me, your heavenly Father.

Exod. 3:14, Eph. 3:16, Eph. 3:20, Isa. 55:9, John 1:3

Is this the God you have heard about or known? May these pages reveal Him more and more!

₧ ₧ ₧

God within You

Here is a great truth and mystery: I am in you, and you are in Me. Regard My presence in your innermost being. Ask Me about the perplexities you face. I will reveal My desires, plan, and purpose for you! Listen for My voice. Do not be distracted by the noise all around you. Many sounds clamor for your attention and drain your time. But not My voice. My voice only enriches your life. You recognize it because you are Mine. So, take My hand and walk with Me. Trust Me. Rely on Me to bring to your attention that which is important. Rest in knowing that the answers are within you because I am within you. I have every solution and connection you need. Simply invite Me to intervene on your behalf. Whatever the circumstance, My voice will guide you. Walk confidently in Me, and My joy will be yours. The result? A cheerful, victorious life!

John 17:20–22, John 14:23, Eph. 3:16, 1 Sam. 30:8, Dan. 2:22, Isa. 30:21

What adjectives would you use to describe the indwelling of God?

ॐ   ॐ   ॐ

The Self-Revealing God

As long as you live, you will wonder and have questions about Me. You have some now. You long to see Me in new and fresh ways—and you can! I continually reveal Myself, not necessarily as you expect Me to, but as I am and as you most need to know Me. I am the heavenly Father who loves you and cares about every detail. As your friend and confidante, I share in your experiences and offer My wisdom. You say, "Show me Your face!" and I do, willingly. But pay close attention. Stay alert to My presence and movements so you can see My glory, power, and dominion. Dwell as deeply as you desire in My holy presence—yes, while you are still in this mortal flesh. I will awaken your spirit and revive your fallen nature. Let Me cleanse you from anything that keeps you from fully occupying your seat in heavenly places. Stay close and I will show you Myself and set you free!

2 Cor. 4:6, Heb. 1:3, Ps. 16:8, 1 Chron. 29:11, Jude 1:25, Isa. 55:1, Rom. 8:11, Eph. 2:6

Is God hiding Himself from you, or are you withdrawing from Him?

ও ও ও

Eternally Good

Dear one, through all eternity I am good, even before time began! Just as a king extends his scepter, inviting His subjects to enter his presence, I extend My goodness and invite you to share in My bounty. Many do not recognize the goodness that comes from Me. They receive My provision without acknowledging its source, never honoring, praising, or thanking Me. Though I am grieved to see them engrossed in themselves and their "getting," My goodness never wanes. Instead, I search for those who express their gratitude, rejoicing My heart and causing Me to fill their hearts with joy. This is the secret of a happy life: to give thanks in everything! Keep it in mind, as My Son did. Discover for yourself the satisfaction, contentment, and peace that come from your gratitude and praise. Praise Me for every blessing you receive, and you will experience even more of My goodness.

Ps. 145, Esther 4:11, 2 Chron. 16:9,
1 Thess. 5:18, 1 Cor. 2:16

*What do the words **eternally good** mean to you?*

 හ   හ   හ

Faithful, Always

In your best and worst times, I am faithful. Yield to Me and invite Me into your situations. I will come in surprising ways! Your human nature wants to quantify Me and process your concerns intellectually. My approach is higher and not always what you expect. My ways are different and My faithfulness is not easily analyzed. It is not what I perform; it is who *I am*. You can rely on Me to carry you through every experience, if you will only ask Me. I am not passive. Whatever the need, I am responsive and engaged. When you are on life's mountaintops, I am faithful. When you tumble into valleys of despair, I am faithful. Let Me encourage you and lift you over every obstacle. Don't expect My faithfulness to mimic what friends and loved ones can do. My faithfulness is of a divine order. No situation, disturbance, or tragedy is beyond My reach. *Receive* My faithfulness, and walk with Me into victory!

Deut. 7:9, James 4:8, Isa. 55:9, Matt. 7:7–8, Ps. 139:7–10

Where do you need God's faithfulness? Will you invite Him in?

ಜ   ಜ   ಜ

My Heart Beats for You

My loving arms are around you even now, drawing you close to My heart, which beats for you. The more aware you are of its rhythm, the more peace and serenity you enjoy. Become enraptured in My presence and all your cares will fade from view. Learn the secret of abiding in Me. Cast your whole being and every concern on Me. Let me enfold you and demonstrate My perfect love. I long to be your *all in all.* Just continue with me and forbid the day's toil to divert you from My presence. Keep maturing in this. Be astute in bringing Me into every situation and circumstance—not as your last resort but your first response. Allow Me to work on your behalf to bring about the desired end. How I love and appreciate your coming to Me! I always hear your cries. I listen and move on your behalf to assist and strengthen you. Never forget that My heart beats for My beloved.

Ps. 16:11, John 15:4, 1 John 4:18, Luke 8:7,
Matt. 11:28, Exod. 22:23

Is it possible to be unloved by the one who so skillfully created you?

ತು   ತು   ತು

Walking with You

Do you feel alone? You aren't. As surely as I created you, I am with you. Even when life is turbulent, I guide your steps. Listen for My voice. I will lead you in the right paths. Just as you come alongside those who are grieving, I walk alongside you and surround you with My love. Just as you bring the hurting to me in prayer, others do the same for you. As you pour out your encouragement, you reap encouragement. Some of it comes directly from My lips to your ears; some comes through those around you. Regardless of how My love is manifested, it will enfold you. Bask in it. Play in My presence the way children play in the safe company of their daddies. Then, as your hope and strength are replenished, you can walk in My grace and power toward what's next. Draw from the resurrection life that raised My Son from death, and let it flow through you to others. This gladdens both our hearts!

John 8:29, Ps. 37:23, Isa. 28:23, Ps. 23:3, Luke 6:38

Do you feel unable to take another step? Ask your heavenly Father to reveal Himself to you.

೮৩   ೮৩   ೮৩

Light to Your Path

Your path is more than a route from here to there. It is the place you are called to rest and thrive. The secret is to place all your cares and anxieties in My hands so I can work on your behalf. Then you are free to prosper, knowing that I am pulling for you, My child and heir. My ear is attuned to your every thought, even the hidden desires of your heart. Nothing escapes My attention. The light of My glory removes the debris from your pathway and uncovers rare treasures within you, even pearls of great price that are not yet unrecognized. My *kingdom* is within you. Walk circumspectly before Me. Allow Me to work in your heart and free up your progress. You are precious to Me. I light your path gladly! Do not forget this, even when the enemy tries to disparage this truth. Yes, there is warfare along the way, but hold fast. Cleave to Me and I will lead you to victory. This is My desire.

1 Pet. 5:7, Rom. 8:31, Rom. 8:17, Luke 17:21,
Ps. 27:1, 119:105

*If your path is covered with debris, who will make it
clear again?*

ಬಿ ಬಿ ಬಿ

God of the Details

Every detail of your life is known to Me. Nothing escapes My attention or seems unimportant to Me. Every detail contributes to a result, and I know the end from the beginning. Let Me help you master the details so your decisions are both sound and empowering. Yes, your reasoning skills are important; but your reliance on My Spirit is crucial. Entrust Me with the little things. Ask, "Father, what are You saying in this situation? Speak, for Your servant is listening." My command of the intricacies is total. Why not surrender your need for control? You cannot control everything; to attempt it is counterproductive. Simply allow Me to perfect My will in and through you. Submit to My care and I will handle your concerns. Voice your praise and adoration. Magnify My name and your life will bring Me glory! Let My tenderness draw you close. Open your heart, and I will make it whole.

Matt. 6:25–34, Isa. 46:9–10, Zech. 4:6, Prov. 14:12,
1 Sam. 3:10, Ps. 138:8

Are you ready to place the troubling details of your life in your Father's care?

ဢ ဢ ဢ

Faithful to Carry You

If you are Mine, I am also yours, and My faithfulness becomes the foundation that upholds your life. Nothing can shake it. Have you forgotten the many times when My steadfast love saved you from trouble? I am always ready to extend My hand to you. I long to lead you. I stand ready to carry you through every trial. Let Me see you to the other side. No matter whom or what disappoints you, I will stand by you. Just remember to walk reverently before Me and heed My instruction. Allow My faithfulness to flow toward you in the everlasting love that My devotion reveals. Continue to trust Me, and you will not only outlast the storm, but you will perform exploits you never imagined—and you will do them in My strength. Simply stick with Me. Stay in My peace. Abandon yourself to My care. Let Me deliver you into all that I have prepared ahead of time. It is yours for the asking.

Ps. 95:7, Matt. 7:25, Isa. 46:4, Isa. 43:2,
Heb. 10:35, Eph. 2:10

Are you trying to carry yourself through a crisis? Will you trust the Father to carry you?

ಬ   ಬ   ಬ

Your Wisdom and Understanding

I am your wisdom, and our time together is precious to Me! It is sheer joy to impart My wisdom and fill your spirit man. Yes! My wisdom is yours for the asking. Simply set yourself apart in silence and rest in Me. Approach the portals of heaven, and you will hear faint whispers. Listen closely; these promptings are heard only when you are present to Me, your heavenly Father. How easy it is to come away with Me! And how close we become when you attentively bid Me to address your concerns. I long to counsel you. I desire to share My heart. So, desire Me! Open yourself to My entrance. I will disclose My wisdom, and My understanding will transform your life. Yes! I will bless you with everything that pertains to life and godliness, enriching you but adding none of the sorrow that worldly riches bring. I am your wise and exalted King, your Father, and teacher. Come learn from Me.

1 Cor. 1:30, Prov. 8:30–31, James 1:5, Matt. 10:27, Isa. 11:2, 2 Pet. 1:3, Prov. 10:22

Where in the Bible have God's people asked for wisdom?
What were their outcomes?

ຂວ ຂວ ຂວ

Your All in All

Yes, *I am* the loving Father who cares for you, utterly and completely. Everything My Word says about Me is true. My attributes are good, and My image-bearers share them and enjoy their fruit. You need only open yourself to receive. My Word reveals Me as your ultimate need and discloses My name, *El Shaddai*, the God who is "more than enough." This is who I am, and I alone can meet your needs. Your soul begs to be filled, not with material goods, fame, or power, but with Me. Only I can complete you. Only I can give you rest. No one else can provide the fully-satisfying, never-disappointing relationship I offer—no one! When I became your heavenly Father and you realized the significance of our new relationship, you overflowed with joy. For the first time, you sensed the wholeness I intended for you. Yes, I am your all in all. And I am more than enough!

Rom. 1:20, Gen. 1:26–27, John 6:50–58, John 15:5,
Gen. 17:1, Deut. 8:3, Matt. 5:6

When you look below the surface of your desires, what or whom do you find?

ও   ও   ও

Faithful When You Doubt Me

Walk with Me and discover My steadfast love. Call on My name and I will care for you! Whatever the hour or issue, My ear is inclined toward you. Tell Me your concerns. Petition Me for your needs. I am your perfect Father, aware of all you face and sure to respond in the most beneficial timing. Often, you forget that I have your best interests at heart. You worry that I am not listening. You wonder whether I care. Yet deep down, You know your fears are unfounded. You know that even if I delay in answering or respond in an unexpected way, I will keep you safe. Rest assured that My actions are governed by My love. Therefore, My goodness is seen when your deepest needs are met in My divine order. Listen closely, for I speak. You know My voice. Let it comfort You, and all doubt will flee.

Ps. 136:1, Jer. 33:3, 1 Sam. 1:27, Matt. 6:8, Eccles. 3:1,
Ps. 34:17, Eph. 3:20, John 10:27–28

Are you letting your doubts stop you from praying, or will you pray about your doubts?

ॐ   ॐ   ॐ

God, Your Shield

I've got you—front and back. Yes! I walk ahead of you and behind you at the same time; I am your defender. In Me you are sheltered from harm. You have accepted My Son's sacrifice; therefore, His blood arrests the enemy's assaults. I am the Good Shepherd. I care for My flock and know each sheep by name. Your fears are not hidden from Me. I know what they are and how they came to be. Before something happens, I know how you will respond. You entered My fold and allowed My presence to surround and animate you. Engage Me more and more. Be My blessed witness. Testify of My care and goodness. Be a sign of My devotion to My children. Walk in the fullness of My glory and power. Remember that I am your shield. Allow nothing to pierce our relationship, and you will not be pierced. Continue walking in love, peace, and My counsel. Worship Me, your protector!

Isa. 52:12, Ps. 33:20, Ps. 91:1, 4, John 10:11, Ps. 139:1-4

How does the Father's protection alter the equations in your life?

ALONE WITH GOD

Ourselves, through God's Eyes

As we discover how God sees us, we see ourselves in a more accurate light. Because He never changes His mind, we can trust what He says! How encouraging it is to know that He is not fickle, as we are. When He says we are the righteousness of God in Christ Jesus and His resurrection life is in us, we can take His words to heart. If we are His, we are loved, appreciated, forgiven, accepted, and chosen as His sons, daughters, and joint heirs. We are seated with Him in heavenly places.

Yes, we can believe it! Most of us have questioned the good things He says about us. We do not always feel loved and appreciated, forgiven and accepted by God. Even as believers, circumstances can tempt us to see ourselves in less-than-affirming ways. That is, until He reminds us of His glorious healing and affirming truth!

Mal. 3:6, Heb. 13:8, 2 Cor. 5:21, Rom. 8:17, Eph. 2:6

જી   જી   જી

My Child

If you have placed your trust in My Son and His sacrifice, I am your Father and you are My child. I know you inside and out, from the number of hairs on your head to the thoughts deep in your heart and the things that bring you joy. My love for you is perfect. Trust Me. I am well acquainted with your desires. I planted them in your heart and will satisfy them as you walk in My abundant grace. Stay close to Me, beloved. Let My love invade your heart and flow freely to everyone you meet. Lean on Me and discover My never-ending supply. By faith, place your hopes in Me and you will enter My joy. You are My child, but not by happenstance; I *chose* you and will cover you. Wrap yourself in Me. Keep your eyes on Me. When you feel brave and when your courage falters, take My hand. I take care of My children.

Rom. 8:15, Gal. 4:6, Matt. 10:30, Ps. 139:2, Ps. 37:4,
1 John 3:1, 4:18, John 15:16, Ps. 55:22

*If you learned early in life to distrust your earthly father,
ask for your heavenly Father's grace to trust Him.*

ಐ   ಐ   ಐ

Apple of My Eye

You are the apple of My eye. I see you, not as you see yourself, but as you are. I know the value I have placed within you, but you are not fully aware of it. You fail to recognize the gifts I supply because they flow from you so naturally. You honor Me when you use them to benefit others, encouraging and building them up in the faith. You bless Me when, by sharing the resources I give, you become a resource to others. You are highly favored! Allow Me to mature you and make you a giant in My kingdom. Walk by faith and let Me care for you. Trust that I am present and working all things for your good. Do not be discouraged when I withhold what does you no good. Keep following after My heart, choosing to please, seek, and know Me. Do you not realize how I prize you? Just think about all that My Word says about you. Then you will believe that you are the apple of My eye!

Ps. 17:8, Zech. 2:8, 1 Thess. 5:11, Heb. 13:21, Heb. 6:1, Ps. 84:11, Rom. 8:28

Is it hard to believe God's high opinion of you? Is your life made harder by doubting it?

೭೦   ೭೦   ೭೦

The Real You

Why, when people speak highly of you, do you cringe, just a little? It is because they see in you what you cannot see in yourself. Their words are encouraging *and* instructive—a reflection of My appraisal. You needn't be so hard on yourself. Absorb the light of My pleasure. Permit My love to seep through your heart and soul. Refuse to let the enemy's words define you or steal your joy. No, you're not perfect; but your flaws do not disqualify you as My child. Bring your shortfalls—whether real or imagined—to Me and I will resolve them. Meanwhile, continue to glorify and praise Me. Remember that you are the apple of My eye. I love you, and others love you. Walk in the riches of that love. My Son died for you. Accept His sacrifice and My approval of you is sealed. Leave your flaws with Me and let *the real you* come alive!

Eph. 2:8, Matt. 5:14, 2 Cor. 5:17, John 15:16,
Eph. 2:10, 1 Pet. 2:9

If you have not yet committed your life to Christ, now is the perfect time! (Please see Preface.)

๛   ๛   ๛

Righteous in Christ

If you have embraced My Son as your Savior and Lord, you are righteous in My eyes. You did nothing to deserve it, and you could not earn it. His righteousness was imputed to you because of His sacrifice, not yours. The free gift of redemption came at a great cost: My Son poured out His own blood. By it, you are made holy, sinless, pure, and healed in My eyes—not in the sweet by and by, but *now*. Earnestly desire the maturity to see yourself this way. Don't let random or habitual thoughts distort your sacred identity. Stand before Me attesting—not arrogantly, but confidently—that you are the righteousness of God in Christ Jesus! Choose to see yourself as I have described you. Let My words take root deep in your spirit so you can become who you really are. Develop this internal picture so clearly that it transforms your life and animates your relationship with Me! In this, I am pleased!

Rom. 4:5, Eph. 2:8–9, Rom. 5:15, Eph. 1:7, Rom. 3:21–22,
2 Cor. 5:21, Rom. 8:15

Is it humble to deny that you are righteous in Christ?
Or is it prideful?

৪৩ ৪৩ ৪৩

Being Perfected

Beloved, accept your humanity and its inherent flaws. Only My Son was perfect. Because of the Fall, you cannot be. Your motives are sometimes tainted. You suffer brokenness. Your personality is imperfect. So, I came with My balm of Gilead to mend and restore you. When you gave Me your heart, you were made new. My Word and Spirit began ministering to you, conforming you more and more to My image and likeness. You came to Me with excess baggage, but My love helps you leave it behind. Yes, you are learning and growing, even now. Our relationship is a work in progress, but as you yield to Me, our union is perfected. More ups and downs are ahead, but don't quit! Allow Me to touch your broken places and heal them. Remain faithful and open to My Spirit. Keep running the race. The prize of the high calling of God in Christ Jesus is yours.

Rom. 3:23, Luke 1:35, Jer. 46:11, 2 Cor. 5:17, Phil. 1:6, 3:14

Are you content to be a work in progress? How does your life demonstrate your contentment?

ઍ ઍ ઍ

Worthy of Forgiveness

You ask, "Lord, why is my spirit broken?" Why, indeed? You received the sacrifice of My Son and you promptly confess your sins. Therefore, you know that I have forgiven you. But will you forgive yourself? Beloved, you condemn yourself for decisions made long ago. You distrust the fullness of redemption, and you subject yourself to untenable standards. This foments inner turmoil. Just accept the wrongs you have done. Throw off the anchors of self-condemnation and self-loathing only exacerbate your grief. Set sail in the wind of My grace. Enjoy the forgiveness you receive. Refuse to carry any burden that My Son has already borne. Be afraid only of hindering My grace with futile works. Accept My love and expect glad surprises. Remember: all things are possible to those *who believe*. So, believe and be free!

Prov. 18:14, Rom. 6:4, 1 John 1:9, Ps. 51:3,
Heb. 12:1–2, Mark 9:23

Are you hindering God's grace by trying to pay for your sins? Are you ready to forgive yourself?

ಬಿ   ಬಿ   ಬಿ

Person of Purpose

The number of your days is known to Me alone. Rest assured that I am not finished with you yet. All that I pour into you serves My eternal purpose and is meant for sharing. So many need what you carry, including My wisdom and grace, which have no expiration date. Keep on giving them away. They are always fresh and potent, able to give life and make people whole again. Yes! My transforming power is *within you*. Don't dismiss it or sell it short. After all, you have experienced it and seen it working in others. Let it go forth in glory, strengthening believers and calling the lost to Me. Let it demonstrate My love through the power of My Spirit. Meanwhile, stay alert to My voice. Watch as I direct your steps through uncertain times. I will not fail you. Simply walk in My love, and all things will work for your good and the good of others. Let that be your legacy!

Ps. 139:16, Matt. 10:8, Eph. 3:20, Phil. 4:13, John 12:32, Prov. 3:5–6, Rom. 8:28

Do you believe God's power works through you? How is it manifested?

ଚ   ଚ   ଚ

My Tenderhearted One

How I delight in the humble heart of one who hears My voice and honors My desires! I'm not looking for a show of mere outward appearances, but for the authentic love that oozes from the tender heart. Yes, you have headstrong moments, and—*yes!*—they lead you into more difficulty than you bargain for. But soon enough you discover that you cannot kick against the goads. As you learn these lessons, your heart is tenderized, becoming more apt to yield. Remember: it was the realization of your need that opened your heart in the first place. Admit your needs to Me now. In this, our relationship becomes more intimate and trusting. You know all things exist in Me, so come to Me. Honor Me with your praise and adoration! I am pleased with your testimony and your witness. When you bow to Me as your Lord, you reveal your gentle spirit. Continue to grow in humility, tenderhearted one, and you will experience more of heaven on earth.

Ps. 25:9, 1 John 3:18, Acts 9:5, Ps. 119:81,
Col. 1:16, Eph. 4:32

How does your life reflect a tender heart?

ಬ   ಬ   ಬ

My Seeker

Beloved, I take pleasure in your pursuit of Me. Keep pressing toward the destination I envision for you. Remain pliable as My goodness graces your life. Though you wonder at times and hesitate along the way, I am there, upholding you. Breathe deeply and lean on Me. Manifest My truth with every step. Know that you will always be learning about the walk of faith that trusts My guidance and relinquishes all other agendas. All the while, you are learning to live in the present, not fretting about the past, which you cannot change, or worrying about the future that is in My hands. Rest in Me. Trust Me. Walk and talk with Me. Listen, and I will direct your paths. Enjoy each moment, knowing I will not fail you. Keep seeking Me, beloved. Nothing pleases Me more!

Prov. 8:17, Phil. 3:14, Isa. 41:10, Ps. 86:11, Prov. 3:5, Prov. 16:25, Matt. 6:34, Ps. 31:14, Isa. 55:3

When life presses, do you shift from seeking God's face to seeking His hand? What adjustments will you make?

ও ও ও

Appointed and Anointed

I have appointed and anointed you. The more you yield to My instruction, the more fruitful you become. Receive My Word as your sustenance. Allow Me to work in your heart more and more, so you become an example of My faithfulness and might. Like the deer who pants for water, come and drink deeply of My Spirit. Drink all you want of Me, but remain thirsty. Continue to feast on Me, and I will satisfy your soul. Know that you can do nothing without Me, so keep suckling at My breast. Let all of the Spirit's fruit be evident in your life. Exhibit My love, joy, peace, faithfulness, gentleness, meekness, goodness, patience, self-control. These are yours; flow in them! Continue to abide in Me. Let Me do the work in you so you can become all that I intend. Continue walking by faith, knowing that I have chosen and empowered you to serve in My name.

1 Pet. 2:9, Ps. 78:1, Jer. 15:16, Ps. 42:1, Isa. 55:2–3,
John 15:5, Gal. 5:22–23, John 15:4

How does knowing that God chose you affect your identity?

ॐ   ॐ   ॐ

Learning to Trust

Each and every day, you face complex situations involving other people. Because you are Mine, My compassion is in you. My discernment is too. Use them both and you will know whether I am directing your steps or you are acting on your penchant for doing good. In this, you will learn to trust My voice rather than your drive to get the job done or the issue settled. Wait patiently for My input. Rest in Me. Your intellect is marvelous. *I gave it to you!* Yet I never intended it to be your primary source of guidance. Only My voice utters perfect instruction. When you heed it, you are walking by faith and pleasing Me. So be encouraged! You are more aware of these distinctions than ever before. Keep it up! Keep walking in the Spirit and relying on My direction. I will never forsake you, and I will always inspire the best outcome for everyone involved.

Isa. 41:13, 2 Tim. 4:5, Prov. 4:20, Ps. 27:14, 1 Sam. 12:22

In trying to "do good," have you ever gotten ahead of God? What was the result?

ৎ৹   ৎ৹   ৎ৹

My Glory Reflected

You might not realize it, but My glory shines through you and affects the atmosphere around you! The glory is not yours, but Mine. You carry it because of your relationship with Me. Our shared love releases My glory and the fragrance of My abiding presence. Bask in My presence, becoming actively saturated with Me so that your spirit harmonizes with Mine. Watch as My glory is manifested through you. Become perfectly attuned to Me as My Spirit fills you and leads you in My ways. My glory is purposeful; it bears witness to My life in you. It is the evidence the world desperately seeks. Do not diminish or nullify its power. Let it arise and shine, and it will cause many to bless My name. They will see plainly that you are Mine, and they will hunger and thirst for My righteousness.

Exod. 34:29–30, 2 Cor. 3:18, Hosea 14:4, John 16:13, 2 Cor. 9:10–11, Matt. 5:6

How is God's glory revealed in and through your life? When are you most aware of it?

೪೦ ೪೦ ೪೦

Attuned to the Invisible World

Remember that I reach out to you despite your unworthiness. Without reservation, I extend My mercy and hold you to My breast. Yes, that is your place with Me—to be close enough to hear the divine heartbeat. Receive all of what I give you as My gift. This is how you function in ways that defy human understanding. By My Spirit, I have given you power and authority to see the invisible world. Become increasingly attuned to it. Before you surrendered to Me, you lacked this kind of vision; but now you can distinguish between earthly and heavenly realms. All of this, because you chose to serve Me as your Lord and Master! I rejoice over your decision. I am with you wherever you go. Press into Me. Let Me guide your journey in the invisible realm. Live victoriously—not independently, but dependent upon Me. Take My hand and rest in Me. I have your best interests at heart and will carry you to the finish line!

Rom. 5:8, Job 32:8, 1 Cor. 2:12, Luke 10:19,
Eph. 1:18-19, Ps. 37:7

*What questions do you have about the invisible world?
Ask Him!*

 හ   හ හ

Generous Heart

An open and generous heart is evident to others, reminding them of Me. As a manifestation of your gratitude, a generous heart seeds the atmosphere with My presence. As you honor Me, your heart becomes more generous, making room for more blessing to enjoy and share. You are revolutionized from within, so that others can also be transformed. This is abundance at its best! Your generosity fuels their gratitude, which inspires *them* to give. Know that faith is working in this, so that the closer you draw to Me, the more deeply you trust in My generosity. The deeper your trust, the more faithful you become. As you allow Me to flow through you into every situation, you experience My *inexhaustible* supply. This is real living! Keep your heart open to the opportunities I present. Lean on My guidance and direction. Let My Spirit be a fountain that flows from you liberally.

Ps. 65:9-13, Ps. 71:8, 2 Cor. 4:15, Heb. 11:6,
James 1:2-4, Prov. 11:24-5

*Does the term **inexhaustible supply** give you hope or raise questions? God is not offended by questions. Just ask Him!*

ℰ ℰ ℰ

Know Me; Know Yourself

Beloved, your hopes and dreams are from Me. I deposited them in you. They are part of who you are—a uniquely called human being. Remember: I have given you all things pertaining to life and godliness. Understand therefore that you cannot know yourself without knowing Me. Settle this truth in your heart and allow Me to work in you. I will reveal the depths of your authentic identity in Me. You have already seen that, as you yield to Me, your identity becomes clearer and more profound. After all, you are My handiwork, and I understand what I create. Never doubt My presence or My hand; I have been with you in and through every experience and event. Learn about Me and move forward from glory to glory. Keep tapping into My wisdom and clarity regarding My plans for you. Your hopes and dreams are My hopes and dreams. They are yours to fulfill!

2 Pet. 1:3, Eph. 2:10, Ps. 139:1-6, 7-10,
Jer. 29:11, 2 Cor. 3:18

Do your hopes and dreams seem to be frustrated? Who will unlock them, and how?

₨ ₨ ₨

Being a Follower

"Follow Me." This is the perpetual invitation of the Light of the world who illumines the darkness and heals the brokenness separating us from ourselves and God. He brings clarity to the human heart, restores wounded souls, and sets them free. For millennia, the Light has mended aching hearts and satisfied their longings. For He knows best what we need. He goes before us, clearing the way, warning us of pitfalls, and revealing the life-giving paths only He can offer. Each and every moment, He entreats us to attend closely to His leading, being obedient and sensitive to His presence and call. The way might be difficult, but if we take heed and are steadfast, He will lead us straight into His will. His words will brighten our paths as we follow Him with open hearts. Receiving His benefits, we can go in peace and confidence, knowing we are His joy and delight.

John 1:43, John 12:26, John 9:5, Ps. 37:4, Matt. 6:8, Ps. 103:2, Zeph. 3:17

₨ ₨ ₨

ℬ ℬ ℬ

Yoked with Me

As change comes and doors of opportunity open, the unknown can stir fear in your heart. Stay in the yoke with Me and I will lead you safely through every passage. Do not fear! The Great I Am is with you—your strength and shield, your high tower in the midst of every transition. Bring Me your burdens and boldly receive My power—an anointing you have not yet experienced. Walk humbly, relying on Me, trusting My heart and My hand. Let Me show you off to those who need My touch. Become My hand extended to them. Don't attempt to figure out what I am doing. Simply accept it and walk in it. Allow Me to bear the load, and you will not grow weary in well-doing. After all, My yoke is easy and My burden is light! Stay joined with Me and the burdens you cling to will lift. You are not called to struggle under their weight, but to cast them off, and follow Me.

John 15:4, Exod. 3:13-14, Ps. 28:7-8, 2 Pet. 5:7, Isa. 58:6, Gal. 6:9, Matt. 11:28-30

Which causes more anxiety—leading or following? Why?

℘ ℘ ℘

Obedient

Many are My gifts to you. Obedience is your gift to Me. Like nothing else, it proves your love. Your eager acquiescence to My promptings and My Word draws you closer to Me and deeper into the privileges of our relationship. Without obedience, the foundation and authenticity of our connection are uncertain. To claim to love is one thing; to show your love is another. Obedience reveals the disposition of your heart. When you obey, I see your commitment and am pleased. I see My heart reflected in your devotion to My will. When you utter a hearty "Yes," you bring Me joy, and you experience even more of My goodness, satisfying the longings of your own heart. How I value your openness to My Word and your agreement with My eternal purpose! How blessed I am by your obedient heart.

Eph. 1:3, Rom. 16:19, Exod. 23:22, Isa. 1:19,
Rom. 6:16–17, Deut. 11:13–15

Have you asked the Father for a willing heart and the courage to obey? Are you committed to following through?

ಙ ಙ ಙ

Open to My Spirit

Beloved, seeing the way you take challenges in stride rejoices My heart. It is not always easy. Sometimes, you become anxious about what will unfold. Because of the Fall, your apprehension doesn't surprise Me. Know this, however: anxiety is not from Me. It is generated in part by the perfectionism that drives you to seek something "better," never allowing you to be satisfied with what *is*. Let Me free you from this bondage so you can reach your destiny unhindered. Trust Me to provide what is best, not what seems most advantageous. Then allow My patience to work in you, denying your rationales the power to control you. This I know: you love flowing with My Spirit. So, speak to your perfectionism and any other contrivance that prevents this flow. Yield your thoughts, actions, and motives to My Spirit, and I will perfect everything that concerns you.

Ps. 147:11, 139:23, 1 Cor. 14:33, Ps. 84:11, Rom. 8:32,
James 1:4, Ps. 138:8

Will you exchange your idea of what is better for God's idea of what is best?

৪০ ৪০ ৪০

Receiving Freely

Beloved, My love reaches into the depths of your being, to your very essence. How pleased I am that you have accepted My love and allowed Me to capture your heart! In receiving My goodness, you have seen many broken places healed. Wherever My Son is received, My balm soothes. Even the most savage heart is softened. My love is offered freely to all, but some reject it. Because you accepted My gift and have stood firm, you walk with Me to this day, displaying My love to others. That is My intent—that you freely receive and then share freely from My supply. Continue walking in My love and I will use you in even greater ways. Keep receiving, and you will never lose heart. Stay the course and do not be dismayed, for I have given you My faith to withstand every storm. Keep looking up, My beloved! Your Redeemer lives!

Ps. 139:13, 1 John 3:1, Col. 1:10, Luke 18:1, Heb. 12:1, Rom. 12:3, Job 19:25

Are you freely receiving the Father's love? Have you said yes to His offer?

৯০ ৯০ ৯০

Giving Freely

Beloved, I have given you every good and perfect gift so that you would bless others. Do you sense My moving upon your heart to reach them and give them hope? It is not a complicated thing. Simply wait for the door to open and share your story. There is no better way to touch a life than to have a conversation from the depths of your heart, and Mine. I am with you and will lead you. You need only be alert for the signs I give you, and prepared to obey. I will not fail you or those you serve. You will be amazed by their responses! This is My gift to you—the power to bless them. Don't let it languish. Make good use of what I pour out! Yes, let it flow *to* you, but also *through* you. That is My plan, and you are My vessel, prepared for this very purpose. Trust My ways and follow Me.

James 1:17, 2 Cor. 1:4, Heb. 13:16, 2 Tim. 4:2, Gal. 6:2, Eph. 4:2, Matt. 10:8, 1 Pet. 4:10

How is your life is affected when you share what God has given you?

෨ ෨ ෨

Eager to Wait

My heart's desire is for you to rely so completely on Me that no disagreement comes between us. I gave you a marvelous mind. I meant it for your good; but how easily it divides us! You have accepted the lie that you must "figure out" everything. So instead of seeking Me, you devise logical solutions to the situations you face. In relying so heavily on your intellect, you rob yourself of My power to turn all things for your good. Instead of consulting Me and seeing what your obedience produces, you preempt My interventions altogether. Beloved, let Me help you. You will find the peace you desire as I come alongside and grace every aspect of your life. Why bear the burden of every decision? Come to Me with your issue. Be eager *to wait* for My solution, and I will glorify Myself in it!

Prov. 3:5, Isa. 55:8–9, Rom. 8:28, Luke 13:34, Ps. 23:2

Are you eager to act on what you know, or eager to wait on God?

ဧ   ဧ   ဧ

Laying It Down

Waiting for Me to work on your behalf is not a natural response. It is supernaturally founded on the belief that I care about your cares and will meet your needs in the most beneficial ways. This proposition rests on My promise that I will do above and beyond *anything* you can imagine. Your role is not passive, however. Your part is to actively place your life in My hands. Lay it down! Express the desires of your heart. Bring your dreams and visions before Me, knowing that My Son is already interceding for you at My right hand. Relish the place of your submission. Acknowledge Me as your sole source of supply. I am not competing with you for control; I am asking you to limit your reliance on your finite ability so I can release My infinite resources. Go ahead, beloved. Enjoy the rewards of My unfettered intervention in your life!

Ps. 130:5, 40:1, 81:10, Eph. 3:20, Heb. 7:25, Acts 2:34

*Have you settled in your heart the Father's promise to
care for you?*

ℬ ℬ ℬ

My Beacon

My glory rests on My disciples. Like a beacon on a
hill, My glory gets people's attention. Some recognize
its gravity and seek to understand more. Others are
only mildly curious and less inclined to press in. This
group runs the risk of being momentarily disrupted but
essentially unchanged. True seekers, however, discover
the empty places in their hearts and drink deeply of My
living water till they overflow with joy. Be aware,
beloved, that transformational moments are not always
clear-cut. The mere fact that people are drawn to you
can be a sign of something stirring deep within them—
something they fail to identify. Do not be discouraged
by their seeming disinterest. Be a good soldier and stay
on your watch. Allow Me to draw them to Myself. Let
My faith, hope, and love flow through you to ignite a
fresh hunger, so that those who are mildly curious
become ravenously hungry for Me. You are My beacon!

2 Cor. 3:18, 1 Cor. 2:14, Job 15:31, Isa. 41:29, John 7:38,
2 Tim. 4:2, 1 Cor. 13:13

In what unexpected ways has God used you?

ॐ ॐ ॐ

Born for This

When you were born, My heart leapt. Not only did I love you, but I knew that you would love Me too. Even now, I rejoice when you turn to Me in hope. I love how you cherish our time together and expectantly listen for My gentle voice. Keep coming to Me; I will deposit more and more blessing in your life. Stay alert! I am doing many new things in you and in the world. You will not miss them, as long as your ear is inclined toward Me. Remain sensitive to My presence, and you will be a testimony of My saving grace, My love, and My keeping power. Walk worthy of your calling, beloved. Look not to the right or the left. Keep your eyes fixed on Me and soak in My unfailing love. Delight Me and I will delight you! My beautiful child, you were born for this.

Ps. 139:17–18, Micah 7:7, 1 Kings 19:12, Isa. 55:3, Acts 1:8, Eph. 4:1–3, Deut. 5:32

Keeping God's Word in mind, imagine the Father's pleasure in giving you life.

ಬಿ   ಬಿ   ಬಿ

Pray Anyway

What is prayer? It is your conversation with Me, your heavenly Father. For those who enjoyed loving relationships with their earthly fathers, conversing with Me is a simple matter. They are accustomed to telling their dads how they feel and what they need. Coming to Me is natural for them. That is not true for everyone. Many are fatherless or feel distanced from their fathers. Therefore, they struggle with prayer. Is that you? Do you withdraw from Me because of your family history? Do you feel stuck there? You needn't be. Remember that your earthly parents did their best with what they had. Even if they failed you, I did not; and *I will not.* You and I have a clean slate. Set aside your misgivings about fathers. With abandon, pour out your heart to Me. It might seem difficult at first; but if you will pray anyway, I will prove Myself worthy of your trust. And I will answer your prayers!

Phil. 4:6, Col. 3:21, Ps. 27:10, 62:8, 18:6

Will you give your heavenly Father the chance to prove His faithfulness? Will you pray?

ဆ   ဆ   ဆ

Tapping Your Gifts

Beloved, I give gifts and talents to every human being. Some use them and find they are multiplied in the using. Others are so afraid to fail that they bury their gifts, depriving themselves and others of the benefits they were created to produce. Have you forgotten what I gave you? Or have you sharpened your abilities and put them to work? Yes, the latter requires effort. Even the most gifted musician, athlete, laborer, or carpenter must persevere in order to excel. Without this determination, your abilities lie dormant. And when they do, you remain unsure of your giftedness and your future. This kind of insecurity is a devilish deception. I created you with limitless potential. You need only accept the gifts I give, envision their use, and *use them*. Dream it. Proclaim it. Decree and declare what I say about you. You are more talented and valuable than you realize!

Matt. 25:14-30, 1 Pet. 4:10, Prov. 14:4, Gal. 6:9,
Prov. 13:4, 10:4, 12:14

Will you be courageous enough to flourish? What step will you take next?

ℰ ℰ ℰ

Yielded and Unflinching

Hear the heart cry of My servant, Job: "Though He slay me, I will hope in Him" (Job 13:15 NASB). This is the sound of the yielded and unflinching heart! Though he was battered by loss, Job's heart was pure. His trust remained intact. He was refreshingly contrite and humble. When a loved one encouraged him to renounce Me, Job refused. Yes, he was fully human and shaken to his core. He questioned Me and himself. Nevertheless, he was righteous in My eyes—not undaunted by suffering, but untainted in his view of Me. Job let My truth drown out the voices arrayed against him. He was not superhuman, and neither are you. Like Job, you have in Me the power to walk in victory, whatever the circumstances. Choose My voice above all others. Encourage yourself in My goodness. Rise above the chatter and know that you are precious to Me. No weapon wielded against you will prosper. You are Mine. I will uphold you.

Job 1–2, 40:3–4, 2:9, 3:11–12, 20–23, 1:8,
42:4–6, Isa. 54:17

In what ways can you relate to Job? Be encouraged by him?

ಲಿ   ಲಿ   ಲಿ

Dressed in My Mantle

You are a star in My kingdom, clothed in My mantle, an example to believers, and a sign to those who do not yet know Me. Because of My Son's sacrifice, you are free to be everything I intended—a person full of grace and truth, expounding the message of freedom in Christ Jesus. Having heard the gospel, confessed your sin, and experienced the power of the risen Christ and His Spirit, you are empowered to wage the war of life and win the victor's crown. Dressed in the mantle I gave you, you reflect My love, and you lead the wayward toward freedom. The mantle is yours. So, go forth boldly. Plant seed. Cultivate and water the ground I entrusted to you. Bring in the harvest I send. Show the lost and hurting what it means to trust Me. The crown of life awaits you! So does My blessing: "Well done, good and faithful servant" (Matt. 25:21 NKJV). Enter the victors' lane, beloved!

Gal. 3:13, Col. 1:13, Eph. 2:10, 6:10-12,
2 Tim. 2:5, Mark 16:15-18

To be clothed in His mantle, you must be His. Have you put your faith in the Savior yet? (Please see Preface.)

છ છ છ

My Brave Warrior

With My mantle comes My anointing. So, let Me use the gifts and fruit of the Spirit that I gave you. Do not let them lie dormant. Reach out in service, and the windows of heaven will open! Do not be timid or constrained by a false sense of humility that hides My power. Remember: I am with you, empowering you by My Spirit. Keep your eyes wide open and your heart tender. Attend to My voice. Move as I direct you. Accomplish what I ask. Stay in faith, nothing wavering, knowing that I am with you to complete the work. Fulfill My promised miracles, signs, and wonders. Let healings be manifested in My name (which is a strong tower). I am waiting to show Myself strong in the earth. Go forth, brave warrior! Remember who goes with you. With Me, you cannot fail. Serve in peace, keeping My training and admonition in mind. Go, and be thoroughly blessed in your obedience!

Isa. 10:27, 1 Cor. 12:4-11, Rom. 12:6-8, Gal. 5:22-23,
Isa. 30:21, John 2:5, Prov. 18:10, Eph. 6:4

Are you humble enough to be brave? How will your heavenly Father help you?

ALONE WITH GOD

Discovering Real Love

We say, "God is love" but can barely find words to explain the superiority of His love to our own. Human love brightens our faces, stirs our hearts, and enriches our lives. God's love does much more. Pure and transforming, it invades the heart and floods the spirit. It is boundless and powerful, pervading every cell of our beings. We cannot fathom God's love with logic, because it is beyond comprehension. God's love simply *is*. The ultimate act of His love was the cross, where Christ, the sinless sacrifice, took the punishment for our sin—all of it! It was His gift, given to make us whole again in spirit, soul, and body. When we accept His sacrifice, His grace is poured out so that we might rise to every occasion, navigate every change in circumstance and every challenging condition, and become all He created us to be. This is real love!

1 John 4:8, 3:1, 16, 4:10, 2 Cor. 9:18

ಐ   ಐ   ಐ

I Am Love

Beloved, *I am* love. This is true love, the very embodiment of My person. I also give love, freely and spontaneously. It is effervescent, satisfying, and lasting. When you receive My love, you sense it in the depths of your being, bubbling over and forever renewing itself. You receive it from Me and pour it out to others. If My Spirit lives within you, so does My love. It is seen in what you do and say. Sometimes, it meets with resistance in the hardened places of your heart where unbelief maintains a stronghold. When you forbid My love, even inadvertently, you subject yourself and others to unlovable thoughts and actions. However, the more you open your heart to Me, the more freely My love flows, pouring from you like a river to glorify Me and bless humanity. Then you are becoming more like Me, in whom there is no darkness at all.

1 John 4:8, Song of Sol., 8:7, 1 John 4:7, John 15:9-10,
Matt. 19:8, 1 John 1:5

How will you immerse yourself more deeply in the love of God?

ↈ   ↈ   ↈ

The Divine Exchange

How sweet is the exchange of love between My Holy Spirit and your reborn human spirit! When My love enters, your spirit becomes alive to Me. My overcoming presence changes the atmosphere and sweetens every interaction. My love becomes the glue of the unity you seek—the oneness that brings peace, joy, and strength to your relationships. My love in you draws those around you into My fold. Like a magnet, it captures their hearts! My love is your light. When you let it shine, others see your good works and glorify your Father in heaven. Never sell yourself short or underestimate My power to work through you. Let My love in you radiate My goodness to the world. When you least expect it, the environment will be transformed and those who don't know Me will sense My presence. Never concern yourself with results; just be yourself and let Me flow through you to a world in need. In this, others will enter My divine exchange.

John 3:3, 2 Cor. 5:17, Col. 2:13, Eph. 4:1-3,
Matt. 5:16, 2 Cor. 12:9

How deep into the divine exchange will you venture?

ʚ   ʚ   ʚ

Waves of Love

Like ocean waves rolling in continuous rhythm, My love flows through your abiding in Me. You need never wonder whether it is present or available. My love is both, if you will avail yourself of it. Just as breakers soak the shoreline, My love soaks your soul and spirit, reviving you in My presence. It speaks to your heart, assuring you that you are not alone in your journey. Even in the darkest times, My love shines brightly. In fact, My love *never fails* as I extend it to you and through you to others. Share My love liberally! Let it water your relationships with family members, friends, and everyone you meet. Allow My love to illumine their dark places and bear fruit in their lives. Meanwhile, keep practicing My love! That is how you mature and bear even greater fruit. Remember that you are My ambassador. Your "diplomatic role" is to share My love wherever you go.

John 1:4, Josh 1:9, John 1:5, Exod. 15:13, 1 Cor. 13:8, John 15:8-9, 2 Cor. 5:20

Do you long to soak in the Father's love? Ask Him to show you how.

ৡ   ৡ   ৡ

Love and Discipline

Beloved, our relationship begins with the purest form of love, which is My love—the love of acceptance, affirmation, and yes, discipline. My love affirms and fosters trust, honesty, integrity, forgiveness, and mercy. It extends My grace and releases My guidance to fulfill My purpose for you. When discipline is needed to keep you from harm or from harming others, I deliver it, not with a bitter taste, but a gentleness that encourages better ways of being. My correction is timely and constrained, so you can receive it without rebelling. Always, My discipline is born from My love and delivered in a manner that turns away wrath. I know about your weaknesses. I see the temptations that assail you. When you miss the mark, I won't withdraw My love or acceptance. You remain My beloved! I do not condemn you; but I will always urge you toward higher ground, for your good and My glory.

1 John 4:18-19, Ps. 86:15, Job 5:17, Eph. 6:4, Heb. 12:6, Prov. 15:1, Heb. 4:15, Eph. 1:5-6

How does understanding God's approach to discipline make His correction more welcome?

    ɞ   ɞ   ɞ

Wrapped in My Love

There is a level of despair in every human heart. I see it and address it by wrapping My arms of love around you and reminding you of the bright future I have planned. Know that My love will reach you even at your lowest ebb. Let Me comfort you and help you to see the beauty that is all around you. I prepared it for your sake! Don't let the pressures of this life and the limits of your understanding blind you to My goodness. Forbid your despair to keep you from Me! I will continuously pour out My love, forgiveness, and power to you. You *will* overcome the obstacles ahead; simply release yourself to My care. Open your heart and spirit to receive Me in new ways. Instead of trusting your human faculties, give Me the reins of your life. I created you to be wholly integrated within yourself and within My kingdom. You are My child. Remain wrapped in My love.

Ps. 42:5, Jer. 29:11, Ps. 86:13, Eccles. 3:11, Luke 8:14,
Isa. 45:2, 1 Pet. 5:6, Ps. 23:3

Are there hidden areas of despair in your life? Will you give them over to the Father's care?

જ જ જ

Gifts of Love

My gifts of love are sent continually, but only some are received. If you will watch for them expectantly and receive them with joy, you can unwrap and use them for My intended purposes, which will greatly benefit you and those around you. My love instills in you all that you are and all you are yet to become. It is a fierce love! Let it woo you, ignite My passions in you, and soothe your restless soul. Share the gift of My love with others, and let others share it with you! It is a priceless healing balm for a sin-sickened, weary world. Release it and it will release them to become more than they ever dreamed possible. Remain sensitive to My gifts of love and appreciative of them. I craft them with each of My children in mind, so they will flourish in My kingdom and My ways. Honor these gifts and walk in them. Go forward in My peace, power, and love. I am always at your side.

Matt. 22:14, Micah 7:7, Rev. 4:11, Col. 1:15–17,
Ps. 52:8, Jer. 31:25

**How can you become more aware of the "love gifts" the
Father sends you?**

ಬಿ   ಬಿ   ಬಿ

Love Like No Other

My love is not of the human variety, which is here today and failing tomorrow. Mine is changeless, always forthcoming, and present before you become consciously aware of it. At times, you are immersed in My love yet oblivious to it. While you wonder where I am, My love flows in a steady stream to fill the hungry places in your soul. Even when you take it for granted, My love is gracious and eager to meet your needs. It is boundless in its scope, bringing joy and contentment to your life. No other love, however deep and devoted, can restore all your broken places to wholeness. My love is compelling and consequential, both drawing you toward My will and empowering you to fulfill it. So be alert and sober. Let nothing and no one cause you to resist My love or doubt it. Stand fast, cherishing the love that is like no other. Allow it to permeate every cell of your being. Experience Me fully. I *am* love.

John 15:13, 1 John 3:18, Ps. 13:1, 145:8, Hos. 11:4,
Ps. 147:3, Rom. 6:23, 1 Pet. 5:8

Where in your life do you most sense God's empowering love?

ဆ ဆ ဆ

My Empowering Love

Beloved, My love heals even a fractured identity. Allow Me to reintroduce you to your inherent and sacred worth. Remember: I value you so highly that My Son died for you! Yes! Trust My assessment. It is pure, unbiased, and without taint. So, receive My love confidently and watch as I renew your consciousness of whom you *really* are. I will restore your identity to its original state so you can become reacquainted with the *you* I envisioned in eternity past. Rediscover the potency of your gifts, talents, and potential. I gave you the capacity to excel beyond your wildest dreams. That is where My dream for you begins. So, forget what is behind you and press forward in My grace and power. Allow Me to exalt you at the right time, for the sake of My glory. Let Me teach you to hone your gifts and release through them the sweet fragrance of heaven. Come and see how highly I esteem you.

Ps. 23:3, Eph. 2:4-7, Rom. 5:8, Ps. 139:13–16, Phil. 3:13, 1 Pet. 5:6, 2 Cor. 2:14

How will you position yourself to receive God's love at the level of your identity?

ಏ   ಏ   ಏ

Pure Love

Whatever you are feeling, know that I love you with all My heart. Know also that My love is pure. You cannot fathom how pure or understand all that it entails. Yet you sense its power and authenticity. When My love invades, darkness flees. Freedom and abundance flood your heart and life. Cares fall away and you become rapt in My presence, rejoicing in the union we share. Yes, you experience the glory of being complete in Me. Even in hard times, you know that in Me, you have all you will ever need. This is the fullness of My love, and you are walking in it! So, take heart! Abide in Me. Let My love catapult you into the dreams I have made alive in your heart. They will become even more beautiful than you imagined—and I will give you new ones! Go forth in My strength, demonstrating My love to this world. They need Me, just as you need Me.

1 John 3:1, Rom. 8:37-39, 5:5, Ps. 16:11,
1 John 4:21, Rom. 8:19

Have the impurities of human love left you skeptical of God's love? Will you reconsider and receive?

ಬಿ ಬಿ ಬಿ

No Strings Attached

My love is given freely, with no strings attached. I loved you before you worshipped Me. I love you when you have nothing to offer. I love you because I am love. Allow My love to touch you and draw you close. Realize that I am your "heart doctor," and wholeness is found in Me. Only I can heal your brokenness. Only I can take your heart in My hands and recreate it. How many times you have called out to Me, to plead your case and decry your situation! Always, I have responded tenderly, providing what is needed and showing you the path forward. My loving-kindness often overtakes you and generates renewed hope, faith, and vision—even when all seems lost! I'm not luring you in or seeking to extract something from you. I draw you close so you can thrive in this world and subdue every attack of the enemy. You were created for victory, but your victory is found in Me. So, come. Receive My love.

Rom. 5:8, Ps. 16:2, 1 John 4:8, Ps. 34:18, 147:3, Ezek. 11:19, Job 10:12, 1 Cor. 15:57

What about God's love strengthens you the most?

ʬ   ʬ   ʬ

Because of Love

Love is My motive. Because I so loved the world, I gave My Son. Because you opened your heart to My Son's sacrifice and now worship Him as your Redeemer, you are a believer and a witness to those who are skeptical or don't yet know Me. Be loving, as I am. Be joyful, as one who is at peace. Be patient, kind, good, and gentle. Be skilled in self-control. Yes! As you open your heart to Me, these qualities come more naturally to you, radiating My love more fully and freely. Keep following Me! I will show Myself faithful to empower you in this. How My heart rejoices as your heart cleaves to Mine, allowing Me to reveal more of Myself to you *and* through you. Continue on this path! I long to show you much more of My kingdom, not only in eternity, but *in this life*. Continue because of love. Your latter days will far exceed the former and you will leave an eternal mark on the world.

John 3:16, Rom. 10:9-10, Acts 1:8, Gal. 5:22-23, Matt. 5:16, Ps. 18:25, Job 8:7

Are you working hard to show God strong, or allowing His strength to work through you?

ஐ ஐ ஐ

Loving Truly

To love truly is to engage as one. Those who love truly share from the depths of their being, staying close when others would flee and giving generously when it would be easier to withhold. My love exceeds theirs; it is the truest love of all. It is constant, genuine, and unflinching. It is giving, abiding, and never failing. It prevails whether it finds you on the mountaintop or in the valley. It is by My Spirit that My love reaches the heights and depths and everywhere in-between—not only going *with* you, but living *in* you. My love permeates every quadrant of your life and searches out your deepest longings. It abounds toward you from the depths of My heart, never extracting or coercing, but enriching and entreating. My love embraces and empowers you to become all that I created you to be, which is much more than you have yet imagined. Come. Let Me love you truly.

Eph. 5:1–2, Gal. 6:2, Prov. 21:26, Ps. 139:7, 1 Chron. 28:9, Prov. 10:22, Rom. 8:37–39

Will you risk opening your wounded heart to receive the truest love of all?

ജ ജ ജ

The Give and Take of Love

My love is sufficient, satisfying the emptiness you have always known, and filling it with worth and value, plans and purposes, dreams and visions. Walk in My love and reciprocate. Yes! Your love is often tentative and always imperfect. Yet these frailties do not diminish My devotion. I understand your humanity and take even greater pleasure in our give and take, because of it. However lopsided our love might be, it is increasing. So, be free! Express your love the best you can and I will open to you new realms of expression. That is My part—not to add, subtract, or divide, but to multiply. I long to open the windows of heaven and pour out blessings on you! I love nothing better. So, let what love you do have flow from your heart in praise, worship, and adoration of Me. Do this and I will satisfy your deepest needs and desires. Continue in our give and take, and your emptiness will end!

Col. 2:9-10, Ps. 81:10, 139:14, 1 John 3:1, Eccles. 7:20, Heb. 4:15, Eph. 1:3, Mal. 3:10, Acts 16:25-26

What might God say about your efforts to love Him as perfectly as He loves you?

ᘒ ᘒ ᘒ

Intimate with God

The word intimate is weighty. To me, it speaks of mutual desire and an openness that fosters trust. True intimacy eliminates hidden agendas and encourages communication that is honest and truthful, accepting and affirming. It frees both parties to be themselves because they feel secure and unafraid in the relationship. Intimacy rings truest when it is shared with God. There is no putting on of airs, no issue of control, no fear of condemnation. In intimacy with God, you can pour out your heart—even the parts you'd rather hide—and know you are still loved. With a soft word, He will reveal the matter and show you a better way forward. To be intimate with God is to experience true rest and peace, knowing the relationship will hold, and you will never be cast aside. Even on your worst days, your Father roots for you and has your best interests at heart. He is the lover of your soul, your one and only God.

John 17:22–23, Jer. 31:3, 33:3, Song of Sol. 2:10

ᘒ ᘒ ᘒ

ಬಿ ಬಿ ಬಿ

Dwell in Me

Sunlight warms you, but the Son of righteousness melts your hardened heart. Abide in Me. Become acutely aware of My love and grace. Let them saturate our communion. I am yours, as surely as you are Mine. Believe this and you will walk more boldly in the power of My Spirit. Dwell in Me deeply and rise effortlessly above life's storms. Worry cannot overcome you there. From your high perch, you stand in authority over your circumstances and call those things that are not as though they were. Yes! If you are Mine, this power *is* present in you. Cultivate it! Refuse to be burdened by past disappointments and failures. Use the power in your tongue to speak to the present and form your best future. This is how you fulfill My high calling on your life. Rest in Me and bless My holy name. Commune closely with Me and experience fullness of joy. Live in Me, and I will transform you.

Mal. 4:2, Ps. 42:1, Eph. 3:17–19, Isa. 40:31, Luke 10:19, 2 Cor. 10:3–5, Phil. 3:13–14, Prov. 18:21, Ps. 16:11

How does fellowship with your heavenly Father affect your heart of hearts?

ॐ   ॐ   ॐ

In My Chamber

We were destined to dwell together in all the fullness of My glory. You experience this most intensely when, daily, you enter My heavenly chamber. How? Through the portal that opens when your heart, spirit, and mind seek Mine. I know that you long to pass through these gates, into the peaceful yet powerful atmosphere of My chamber. Did you know that My children are always welcome there? Come! Find Me and commune with Me in total rest and harmony. My chamber is that singular and sacred place, that perfect sanctuary where you and I can communicate unhindered—heart to heart and spirit to Spirit. Though you can never fully explain it, you know when you have crossed the seam between the earthly realm and the heavenly one. So, do it by faith and by My Spirit. Connect with Me in ways you did not formerly comprehend. I welcome you to My chamber!

1 John 3:24, 2 Cor. 4:6, Ps. 104:3, 13, Rev. 11:12,
Song of Sol. 2:14

Are you awaiting God's invitation, or have you already accepted it?

ಠ ಠ ಠ

Our Conversation

My chamber. Just the two of us, conversing in a dimension beyond the earth's atmosphere. So, breathe deeply of the heavenly "air," which is My glory, My environment. Approach Me here and My glory will envelop you! You won't want to leave. What we talk about here goes far beyond words. It is life itself, substance that energizes and acclimates you to new dimensions in Me. Why? Because you have seen with your eyes, heard with your ears, and fully experienced the "more" that I have for you. Continue to converse with Me. Seek My glory. Pursue My presence. Boldly and relentlessly invade the heavenly domain. Invoke the opening of heaven's portals so we can continue our conversation. Remain in My chamber. Sup with Me. Let Me refresh and revitalize you with My satisfying presence. Feast on all that I say to you. I prepared it with you in mind.

Acts 17:28, Heb. 4:16, 1 John 1:1–10, Jer. 29:13, Ps. 34:8

How will you seek deeper fellowship with your Father in heaven?

⁊   ⁊   ⁊

Intimate Words

Lean in, beloved, and hear My voice! It is the clarion sound that inspired the prophets of old. They heard Me because they made themselves available. They opened their hearts and embraced My words. My speaking did not end with them; I am still speaking to My people—yes, to you! My words are carefully chosen, and they are intimate by nature. They give you hope, strengthening you and instilling perseverance. Let them encourage your faith, even when you see no way forward. Trust Me! When I speak, the way will appear. When My words pierce your heart, they will prepare you for the future and prepare the future for you! Inhale My words, for they are life and breath to you. *You are hearing from the living God.* Covet My voice. Honor My presence. Listen, beloved, and I will reveal Myself to your deep places. Hear Me and live anew.

Exod. 19:5, Heb. 1:1-2, Num. 23:19, 1 Sam. 3:10,
Isa. 43:16-19, Ps. 33:6, Job 32:8, Jer. 10:10

How do you respond to the Father's voice?

ဆ ဆ ဆ

Search My Heart

Nestle in with Me and search My heart. Let My pure love and your devotion meld, refreshing our relationship day by day. My heart is wide open to you. Have as much of it as your appetite will allow; and then have some more. Let your hunger increase and you will gladden both of us! Cherish our time together and your wounds from the past—even the most painful memories—will be healed. My Son purchased Your restoration. Receive its fullness here, in My presence. Listen for My counsel and embrace My words. I will tell you how precious you are to Me and how I delight in you. Don't take it lightly. I am not puffing you up. Nor is it prideful to receive My affirmations. No. It is prideful to reject them! Cleave to My heart and you will find storehouses of hope, faith, joy, and the resurrection life that raised My Son from the grave. Search My heart, and they are yours.

Jer. 29:13, Ps. 42:1, Isa. 55:1, Ps. 147:3, Isa. 53:5, Prov. 4:20, Isa. 49:16, Phil. 3:10

Is anything hindering your intimate fellowship with the Father? Let Him reveal and heal it.

ᛒ ᛒ ᛒ

Feast on Me

How your mind works to drum up fears and tempt you with contrivances! Will you admit that it is exhausting you? I do not say, "Disparage your mind." No! Value it. But rule over it. Instead of feeding on rationales and "good ideas," come sit at My feet. Feast on all that I am, and find all that you need. My Spirit will comfort you. Your fears will recede. Trust Me with your whole heart. Let your understanding be tested in light of the truth. Follow Me. I will point the way! The enemy seeks a toehold from which to distract and overcome you with fear and worry about many things, most of which will never even happen. Reject his suggestions! Be cloistered in Me, your safe place. Close the door behind you and make this time ours alone. Abide with Me and no demonic scheme can touch you. Simply rest in My presence. I will bathe you in hyssop and refresh you. Feast on Me.

Rom. 8:6, Prov. 25:28, Luke 10:38-42, John 6:56, Ps. 23:5, Prov. 3:5, Jer. 17:9-10, John 10:10, Ps. 91:2

How heartily are you partaking of what the Father is offering in this moment?

ॐ ॐ ॐ

Father and Child

Beloved, our relationship is intimate in its essence. I am your Abba Father, and you are My child. Did your earthly parents fail you? I will not. Did they desert you? I will stay. I have always been with you. I knitted you together in your mother's womb. I know the number of hairs on your head. In the everyday events and in your times of crisis, I am there. Cling to Me. Meditate on My Word. Come into My chamber and leave the noise behind. I am your constant companion. Be candid, transparent, and unguarded—*intimate*. Call on Me in your victories and your blunders. I will give you peace and rest. Be tenacious and straightforward. Do not mince your words. This is your Papa you are talking to! Feel free to bombard the portals of heaven with whatever is on your heart, and I will hear you. Don't back off or couch your requests in flowery words. Be yourself in the presence of your Abba. We are family.

Gal. 4:6, Ps. 27:10, Isa. 62:4, Jer. 1:5, Luke 12:7, Josh. 1:8,
Jer. 29:12, 1 Thess. 5:16–18

How does the Father's promise of unending devotion soothe your wounded soul?

ಬ ಬ ಬ

Precious

Precious to Me is the way you value our time together and remain open to My correction. How you move Me when, without reservation, you give your heart and life, even when tribulation tempts you to take flight. Still you say, "Lord, I am Yours. Do with Me what pleases You." How circumspectly you walk, honoring Me not only for what I do but for who I am. How sublime our intimacy becomes when you lay open your heart to My healing touch and burst forth in songs of praise to Me. Precious are our conversations, the simple but beautiful exchanges of thoughts and words that lead to your deliverance. Yes! They are precious. Let Me continue to form you in My image and likeness, more each day, through My Word and My Spirit. Let Me bring you deeper into the abundant life that satisfies you and glorifies Me. Walk boldly in My promises, great and precious as they are.

Prov. 23:26, Luke 1:38, Eph. 5:15, Ps. 50:23, 62:5, Isa. 64:8, John 10:10, 2 Pet. 1:4

How are the Father, Son, and Holy Spirit precious to you?

ഇ ഇ ഇ

Inseparable

Relax. You are not alone. I am in you, in your midst, and all around you. Whether you are coming in or going out, sitting down or rising up, I am there, listening to your cries and inspiring your dreams. We are inseparable. Your slightest whisper touches My heart. Why do you worry? I am aware of your needs and prepared to satisfy them. Don't run this way and that, chasing solutions that appease your rational mind but forfeit My power. Stay in step with Me, in perfect unison and you will lack nothing. This is the mature walk of faith: releasing yourself to the fullness and power of My will for you. Yield and new vistas of adventure and provision will appear. The more intimately you reveal yourself to Me, the more readily My dreams and visions can satisfy your longings. This is the fulfillment you seek: a life of consecration, led by My Spirit into My perfect will. Inseparable.

John 14:16–18, Jer. 23:24, Ps. 139:1–4, Matt. 6:25–34, Gal. 5:25, James 1:4, Matt. 6:9–10

When do you feel most alone? How might you open that part of your life to your Father?

ৰু ৰু ৰু

Our Adventure

Walking in intimate relationship with Me is a glorious adventure. My blessing makes you rich indeed—in devotion and divine love, in human relationships and earthly commodities, and in your experiences. This is fullness of life! So, take pleasure in My company, bask in My glory, and abide in Me. This is blessing—a life, not of addition or subtraction but multiplication. That is the mark of My presence! Such blessing does not eliminate every trial and challenge; it is discovered even in the midst of your difficulties. That is where you discover the ties that bind us. There you learn to live in the present moment with grace and thanksgiving, enjoying the full arc of your adventure and our shared love. Let My presence invade your life, and My blessing will overtake you. Receive it, even when the road gets rough and you feel undeserving. We are in this adventure together.

Heb. 12:2, Prov. 10:22, Acts 2:28, John 16:33,
James 1:2-4, Rom. 8:28

How is your adventure with the Father teaching you to trust Him more?

ಐ ಐ ಐ

Safe in Me

In My arms of love and grace, you are safe. Draw close to Me. See how your anxiety recedes and your perspective becomes clearer. You feel safe in My care, realizing that you can trust the protection I provide. Rest in Me, where no wickedness or terror can overwhelm you. Though fear beckons, your confidence in My covenant stands firm, and My benefits become increasingly evident. As My goodness overflows, you cannot help but praise Me! Earnestly, you express your gratitude for My faithfulness. Stay centered in Me! Recognize the enemy's schemes to draw you away, and refuse to entertain them. You have My permission—even My mandate!—to be more than a conqueror. Exercise your dominion in this world and enjoy your days *to the full*. My love and grace make this possible. Stay close to Me and you will stay safe. Go forward *with Me* in My presence, promises, and glory.

Ps. 4:8, Job 5:9, Ps. 132:13-15, 91:5-10, 56:4, Job 18:5-7,
2 Cor. 2:11, Eph. 6:11, Rom. 8:37, Prov. 3:2

Contemplate your safety in God. How does it affect your view of life?

ೞ   ೞ   ೞ

Bask in My Love

When issues try to eat you alive, when despair follows close on your heels, pause and bask in My love. To the natural mind, this is counterintuitive. To your born-again spirit, it is life. Let nothing come between us. Trouble will tempt you to put our relationship on hold. Don't do it. Yes, I am jealous for you—for your sake. Let Me minister to your needs. I know you want to isolate when you need Me most. Don't run, My beloved. Stay out in the open. Let's communicate freely. Let the sound of My voice calm your fears and reassure you of My care. Remain vitally connected to Me, dwelling in the deepest folds of our relationship, and I will work out everything that concerns you. I gave you the desires of your heart, and I will grant their fulfillment. You have a personal relationship with the Alpha and Omega, the beginning and the end, the lover of your soul! Pause and think of that!

Ps. 42:5, Heb. 4:9–10, Rom. 8:7, 1 Cor. 6:17, Exod. 34:14,
John 15:4, Ps. 37:4–5, Rev. 1:8

What is attempting to separate you from your Father's loving care? Will you bask in His love anyway?

ଈଃ   ଈଃ   ଈଃ

Here, at My Throne

My throne room is open to you. Bless and honor Me, and there you will abide. Isn't that where you long to be—in My presence? Have you not cried out for Me to order your steps? Yes, I hear your cries and long for you to come, knowing your heart's desire is to please Me. How that makes My heart rejoice! So, come freely, but do not take My presence for granted. Only the continual work of grace frees you to enter My presence and worship Me there. So, make the most of it! Cultivate your hunger for Me so it will flourish and feed your life. Come to Me and My Spirit will facilitate our conversation. See Me with the eyes of your heart. Experience Me. I am real! Enter My invisible world and see that it is more real than the earthly realm. Continue walking by faith. Enjoy My presence and hear My thoughts toward you. Let Me guide and direct your steps. My love is true.

Isa. 66:1, Rev. 3:21, Ps. 42:1-2, 2 Sam. 22:7, Heb. 4:15, Deut. 8:3, Col. 1:15-16, Ps. 139:17-18

Is it hard to believe God's invitation is real? Did He not prove it by sending His Son for our sakes?

ℬ   ℬ   ℬ

Living in and for Him

To live in Christ is to be one with the Savior, thriving in the same resurrection power that raised Him from the grave. Yet, how we resist! Believing that we can "do it ourselves," we shut Him out, miss the glorious exploits He has ordained, and forego the sanctification and grace we can find nowhere else. How our Lord longs to help! How ready He is to provide an exponentially more rewarding life than the meager one we fight to attain. So, He waits until, desperate and clothed only in humility, we lay down the lies that leave us exhausted and empty-handed before Him. Surrendered once and for all, we can live for Him, offering up ourselves and our situations to His care. Without a hint of upbraiding, He guides and strengthens us, and pours out generous helpings of His grace, mercy, and love. Ah! This is real living.

Phil. 3:7–11, Jer. 29:11, Rom. 12:1–2

ℬ   ℬ   ℬ

ဆ ဆ ဆ

Heart Like Mine

Follow Me and your heart will become more like Mine—open, expressive, receptive to others, sensitive to their pain, tender, and compassionate. Walk as a living demonstration of My love amid a crooked generation, sharing My light even with those who seem unwilling to receive it. How powerful your witness is when My presence and glory shine through you! You become an attraction, a cause for hope to the lost. Glow on, beloved! Let no one diminish you or deter you from your assignment. Be alert; your adversary seeks to dilute your effectiveness. Be discerning and in tune with Me. Yes! Call on Me. I will answer you and go before you in battle. Hold your head high. You are a worthy soldier of the cross, keen in battle, astute, and ready for the enemy's assaults. Walk in My victory. Abound in all things. Go in the peace and love that only I can give. Thank and praise Me, and watch what I will do!

John 12:26, 1 Pet. 3:8, Rom. 12:1, John 1:4-5, Phil. 2:14-16,
Col. 1:27, 1 Pet. 5:8, Jer. 33:3, Isa. 52:12,
1 Cor. 15:58, 2 Cor. 8:7

How does your heart most closely reflect the Lord's?

ॐ   ॐ   ॐ

My Passion in You

What is your passion? Is it to encourage others? Assist the elderly? Comfort the grieving? My passion is in you. Pursue it by My Spirit! Hone your skills and let My grace sustain your efforts. I will set captives free— not just them, but you! Simply yield yourself to Me. Don't be afraid of the well running dry. I am the well that never runs dry. Allow Me to flow through you to accomplish My desire on behalf of those I send you. I raised you up to do the greater works I promised. Pray for the sick and look to Me to restore them. Comfort prisoners and see them set free, just as you have been set free. Yes! Bring the lost to salvation through My name. Trust what I have given you. Don't minimize your part or the manner in which I use you. Accept your gifts and My choices. Walk in peace, knowing that you are righteous before Me and deeply loved—a vessel of My passion.

Isa. 58:6-7, 2 Cor. 12:9, Luke 4:18, John 7:38,
John 14:12, Rom. 9:23-24

Are your passions mysterious or unclear to you? Ask your heavenly Father to reveal them.

ಲ   ಲ   ಲ

In You and through You

My hand is leading and guiding you. At times, you recognize it. At other times, you are not consciously aware of My involvement, but mistakenly believe that you are acting on your own idea. Beloved, I put it there. Yes. You have sometimes strayed onto paths of your own making; but I drew you back to the right road. I have sent you across many people's paths and have blessed you in the process. You have also blessed their lives, for the anointing flows through you. Continue to rely on Me to accomplish My purposes in your life and the lives of those you meet. Trust in Me. Be patient and still. Wait in reverence and peace for the desires of your heart to be fulfilled. Look to Me, the author and finisher of your faith as you continue your life's journey. I am with you, working all things for good and for your well-being. Do not be dismayed. What I promise, I will deliver. Follow Me.

Isa. 41:13, Ps. 43:3, 25:4-5, Prov. 11:25, Jer. 29:11,
Ps. 46:10, Heb. 12:2

*How might God be more involved in your life than
you realize?*

ജ ജ ജ

My Desires, Your Adventure

Your heart beats with longings I have placed there—desires, dreams, visions, and prophetic words that speak to all you are becoming. You and I both long to see them fulfilled. Continue to release yourself into My care. Receive the continued healing of your soul. In doing so, you permit the powerful unfolding of all that I have revealed. All of it is possible with Me. My heart's desire is for your life to be a glorious and satisfying adventure that accomplishes My eternal purpose. Keep drawing close to Me. Be absorbed in My presence; practice it and I will provide all life, guidance, and power. Hold to the course I reveal. Keep your eyes on the mark! Let Me be the wind that fills your sails and produces in your heart the forward motion you envision. I am the breath of life within you. You know Me and My voice. Now allow Me to provide every benefit that is yours in Christ Jesus.

Phil. 2:13, Ps. 20:4, 37:4, Joel 2:28, 1 Pet. 5:7, Ps. 23:3, Dan. 11:32, Ps. 16:11, Neh. 8:10, Job 33:4

Do you wonder whether your God-given dreams are possible? Look to Him!

ౠ ౠ ౠ

Look Ahead

Beloved, you have seen the cruelty of the human will and have suffered a broken heart. People you trusted took advantage of you, and some abused you. Though I never promised you a life without struggle, I never fail you in your suffering. My healing balm mends your brokenness. My strength lifts you. My Spirit provides the courage you need to press toward wholeness. Keep going! Don't look back, but look ahead! See My good works in your life. I withhold nothing beneficial from you. At My command, doors spring open. Walk through them! Experience My goodness in the land of the living, always guarding your heart and mind. The assaults of the enemy will come. Be prepared to quench every fiery dart he unleashes. Stay in My peace and move forward. I am with you through every step! Do these things and you will glorify Me. Humble yourself and I will exalt you!

Mark 7:21-23, Ps. 41:9, Matt. 26:21, John 16:33,
Ps. 34:18, 84:11, 27:13, Phil. 4:7, Eph. 6:16, 1 Pet. 5:6

Are you suffering from a broken heart? Have you asked your heavenly Father to heal you?

ဢ ဢ ဢ

Inner Struggle

Beloved, there is a struggle, but not with Me. Your struggle is internal. You are trying to make sense of swirling emotions, feelings of frustration, and external changes that try your soul. You are learning that there can be no peace *without* until there is peace *within*. Such peace is only available by My Spirit, so call on Me! I hear your cries. I heed your pleas and respond from the fullness of My love to provide precisely what you need. Come! Feast at My table. Let My bounty nourish the deepest longings of your heart. Remember: because you have repented and received My Son's sacrifice, your past is forgiven. In fact, it is *obliterated*! I have given you a brand-new heart of flesh, and with it, newness of life. Go forth confidently in My love with new depths of revelation, understanding who you are and the glory that resides in you. I am your rock and your fortress, in all things.

1 Cor. 10:13, Rom. 15:13, Isa. 55:6, Ps. 120:1, Phil. 4:19, Col. 1:13, Ps. 103:12, Ezek. 36:26, Rom. 6:4, Ps. 18:2

Will you struggle forever? Or will you receive what Christ has done for you?

ॐ ॐ ॐ

In My Peace

My peace flows freely, so rest in Me! The peace I give is not what the world gives. Mine is an over-the-top kind of peace that overwhelms your difficulties. Let the gentleness and strength of My peace rule you. Abide in My presence and My peace will follow. It is that simple! Without realizing it, you will become an example to others, and they will want to walk with Me too. Yes, your peace will baffle them; but it will also attract them to Me! They will learn what you are learning: that nothing in this life can force you to surrender your peace, and nothing in this world can compare with it. Know this: My peace is not the absence of trouble; it is My presence and glory flooding your innermost being, so that you can keep standing, whatever the circumstances. My peace will astound you and amaze those with whom you come into contact. Let them witness My goodness, in My peace.

John 14:27, Phil. 4:7, Col. 3:15, Prov. 12:20, 16:7,
Ps. 119:165, Isa. 54:10, 55:12, 9:6

Does peace seem to be in short supply? Seek the Prince of Peace!

ფ ფ ფ

Clay in My Hands

Beloved, through every mountaintop and valley experience, I have been there. Many more experiences are still ahead. Keep clinging to Me and My Word. Neither will fail you. Over time, you have allowed Me to bring a measure of healing and restoration to the broken places in your life. How I long to do more! Let Me melt your heart. Let Me hold you close and fill you with Myself. You are a vessel of honor in My courts, beautifully formed, yet as soft clay in My hands. Yes! You are your Potter's delight, and I have fashioned you after My own heart. See yourself as I do. Accept what I say about you, without hesitation, allowing no *ifs*, *ands*, or *buts* to contradict Me. You are totally forgiven, the righteousness of God in Christ Jesus, cleansed and whole in My sight. You are both perfect and healed, holy and pure. Everything you do prospers. So, walk in My blessing, which adds only joy, and let Me form you.

Prov. 4:20-22, Eph. 3:17-19, 2 Tim. 2:20, Isa. 64:8,
2 Cor. 5:21, Ps. 1:3, Prov. 10:22

Describe your experience on the Potter's wheel.

ೞ   ೞ   ೞ

Courageous Soldier

Take courage—not by drumming it up, but by drawing from Me all you need for the situations and circumstances you face. Remember that all things work together for good to those who are called by Me. Called indeed—out from the crowd and into My extraordinary ways. Take time with Me. Listen and do what I show you. That is My will! Keep walking in the paths of My righteousness, yielding your heart in praise and adoration. Day by day, find yourself more attuned to Me, better able to discern My voice, My heart. Yes! My hand is on you. Others might not see or mention it, but they benefit as you exude My presence. When they are intimidated by My glory, keep moving in Me. Stand as My good soldier, your armor settled, your eyes fixed on Me. My abiding is not fickle. Walk courageously and fearlessly. I am your ever-present shield and buckler, your trustworthy defense.

Ps. 27:14, Isa. 35:4, Rom. 8:28, Zech. 3:7, Rom. 12:1-2,
2 Cor. 1:4, Ps. 36:9, 91:4

Is your courage human or divine?

෨   ෨   ෨

Moved by My Voice

Beloved, keep tuning your ear to My still, small voice. See how sensitive your hearing becomes and how aware you are of My sound. Notice the shift in your demeanor as My Spirit moves. A stillness settles over you, and we commune, often at a level beyond words. Yet you feel compelled to capture the essence of our communion. How it pleases Me when you inscribe My impartations without questioning them, only seeking to record them accurately, as My faithful witness. As I write on your heart, you write with your pen. Always, I have had scribes, including the prophets and apostles of old through whom I delivered My Holy Book. My work through you is both similar and different. Through your writings, I am purifying you, bringing the cohesion you desire so that your mind and spirit work hand in glove to do My bidding. When you are unified within, others see Me more clearly. So, onward, My scribe. Onward!

1 Kings 19:11–12, Gen. 3:8–10, Ps. 45:1, Isa. 8:2,
Ps. 12:6, 1 Pet. 1:7

Describe the voice that moves your heart like no other.

ೞ   ೞ   ೞ

Light in Dark Places

My presence envelops you, even in the dark places. My presence is radiant, attracting others to its brightness and renewing the hope of freedom. The lost suddenly see My part in their lives. They are awakened to My Spirit and drawn away from the spirit of the world. They become alive when they see within themselves what they hadn't noticed before: *the divine image*. Beloved, allow My presence to energize the atmosphere and make holy ground of the place where you stand. Permit My fruit to flow freely, and I will do the work I promised. Simply cooperate. Flow with Me in the atmosphere of My glory. My gifts will restore healing and wholeness to the hurting. Continue to let your light shine, so that even those who never knew Me will rejoice and glorify Me! Light, be!

Ps. 139:7, Luke 9:28-31, Exod. 13:21, Gal. 5:22-23,
1 Cor. 12:9, 28, Matt. 5:14-16, Gen. 1:3

Does letting your light shine seem too risky? Are not His light and power reliable?

❧ ❧ ❧

Song of Joy

Joy bells are ringing in your heart! I have given you a song to feast on. It is the sound of the Savior, everywhere you go. Joy is precious to you, because it is precious to Me. Bask in it! It is your strength. I will refresh it during our times together. It will re-sound in ever more perfect harmony and rhythm—the tones and cadences of our communion together. This is the joy of the relationship we share. Let My presence saturate you anew. Breathe in My Holy Spirit and I will take you to My heavenly abode, where you can escape time and space for a little while. Dwell with Me. In this you are set apart, so I can bless you with Myself. Yes. Others can bless you, but only I can satisfy your deepest longings. Friends and loved ones do their best, and still you are disappointed and left wanting. So, come feast on My joy. Let My joy bells ring. Sing, My beloved!

Ps. 40:3, 47:1, Neh. 8:10, Prov. 10:28, Rom. 15:13,
Isa. 12:6, Rom. 14:17

Which is more lasting: joy or happiness?

ဆ ဆ ဆ

Divine Mysteries

Life is a beautiful, glorious, God-given mystery that is unveiled as you live it. Pat answers cannot suffice. My answers are layered with nuance and understanding. Press into the fullness of the life I gave you, and I will reveal My answers. This requires trust, not in self but in Me—one day, one hour, one minute at a time. So it is for all. Those who rest in their pat answers for even a moment soon find the fruit of their reasoning to be bitter. Beloved, life and death are in the power of the words you choose and the actions that follow. So, choose life! Let My infallible Word guide you and be the yardstick by which you measure all aspects of your life. My truths will nourish and protect you. Eat them! They point to My Son, in whom your life is hidden. What a beautiful, glorious, divine mystery this is.

Job 12:22, 12, James 1:5, Prov. 3:7, 18:21, Deut. 30:19-20, Ps. 119:160, 2 Tim. 3:16, 1 Pet. 2:2, Col. 3:3

Have you begun to imagine the mysteries yet to unfold?
Have you asked God for revelation?

108

ಬು ಬು ಬು

Pour Out My Love

Not a moment passes without My love reaching for you. Receive it. Bask in it. Replenish your stores. Your Father knows how life's cares drain you and attempt to obscure My love. So, be still and know that I am God, and I am love. Let My presence refresh and urge you onward with the reassurance of My presence. Share My love wherever you go. Do not hold back. Keep giving and your supply will never run out. Do you know who is most desperate for Me? Can you always tell? No, appearances can be deceiving. So give My love freely. Lavish it. Be instant in and out of season. Manifest My love and power, and they will reach the hungry ones. Be My open conduit and My sustenance will flow. Search deeply for Me and watch My living water satisfy those you meet along the way. I have given you My own love. Walk in its purity, and My presence within you will shine. Pour Me out to the world!

Ps. 36:5-7, 63:3, Eph. 3:14-19, Ps. 46:10, 1 John 4:8,
Rom. 13:8, Prov. 11:24, 2 Tim. 4:2, John 7:37-38

Are you ready to be a conduit of God's love, always overflowing? Why, and how?

ත ත ත

Deep in the River

The river of life flows from My being, continually, without interruption or end, gentle and mild, robust and active, enlivening all who will take the plunge. When you are ready for immersion, I open its full power to you. So, release yourself to the river's depths and drink deeply. Respect its power, but fear not. This is the rich river of My Spirit. It never runs dry, and it will take you as far in Me as you are willing to go. Yes! It will even take you where I am going. Let My Spirit draw you in again and again. I will fill your empty places and restore your buoyancy. Let the river be your place of renewal. Everything you need is in its waters! So, let it flow in and through you to revitalize and transform you, and renew others. Yield yourself between its banks and take from it all you desire. How I long to share My life with you! Be continually filled, beloved. Linger in the deep waters of My Spirit!

Rev. 22:1, John 4:14, Ezek. 47:1-5, Gen. 26:24, Isa. 44:3, Ps. 65:9, Isa. 55:1, Eph. 5:18

How deep will you go in God?

ॐ ॐ ॐ

My Ambassador

Surrendered to Me, you are part of My kingdom, an extension of My presence endued with power and responsibility. Trust Me in both and I will work in astonishing ways. *Nothing* shall be impossible. Only believe, and I will do it. You are My ambassador. Represent Me. Reveal Me. Glorify Me. Make peace in My name. Use the weapons of your warfare. Accomplish My eternal purpose by completing your assignment. Never be intimidated by the seemingly powerful. There is no power greater than Mine. The Great I AM goes ahead of you. I am also your rear guard. My very Spirit is *in you*. Call on Me. I will keep you. Cast every care on Me. Allow Me to unlock every resistant place. Watch the impossible become possible. Arise to undreamed of heights. Avail yourself of My limitless supply. Remain engaged yet resting in Me as I orchestrate the symphony that is your life. *Live in Me.*

Rev. 12:1, Gal. 2:20, 1 Cor. 3:9, Ps. 29:11, Luke 1:37,
Mark 5:36, 2 Cor. 5:20, 10:4, Isa. 52:12

Your heavenly Father handpicked you to represent His kingdom. Are you consciously carrying the mantle He prepared for you?

About the Author

Alexander Zanazanian grew up in an Armenian home in Philadelphia. He is a first-generation American whose parents immigrated from Turkey in 1925 and 1929. Alexander was raised in the Church. At the age of twelve, he accepted Christ at a farm camp run by an evangelist in Mays Landing, New Jersey. Alexander attended Villanova University and graduated with a degree in mechanical engineering. At the age of thirty-five, he received the second in-filling with the help of Pastor Ed Mooney. Alexander has been on thirteen mission trips in Europe and Central and South America and has served on the boards of several ministry bodies. He first started journaling in 1980 and has enjoyed the practice ever since. He presently attends Church on the Living Edge near Orlando, Florida. Alexander was married to his wife Nancy for sixty years before her death. They have one daughter, Deborah Hilewick, and her husband John Hilewick; two grandchildren, Joshua Hilewick and Stephanie Duddy and husband Scott; and two great-grandchildren, Mckenzie and Teagan Duddy.

Made in the USA
Columbia, SC
31 December 2021